Contents

Adventures
with
Microorganisms

Owen Bishop

John Murray

Other books in the Adventures series

Digital Electronics
Electronics
Microelectronics
Physics
Astronomy
Woodwork
Small Animals ⎫
Small Plants ⎭ by Owen Bishop

By the same author

Natural Communities
Outdoor Biology (Teachers' Guide and 3 Pupils' Books)

Acknowledgement

I am grateful to Norman Parker, of the Biology Department
of Millfield School, for his skill and enthusiasm in producing
the illustrations for this book.

© O. N. Bishop 1984

First published 1984
by John Murray (Publishers) Ltd
50 Albemarle Street, London W1X 4BD

Printed and bound in Great Britain by
Richard Clay (The Chaucer Press) Ltd, Bungay, Suffolk

Set in Monophoto Plantin

British Library Cataloguing in Publication Data

Bishop, Owen
  Adventures with microorganisms.
  1. Micro-organisms
  I. Title
  576   QR41.2
ISBN 0–7195–4074–7   ISBN 0–7195–4075–5 Pbk

What this book is about

The organisms that are referred to as 'micro-organisms' in the title of this book are the extremely small living creatures that are to be found in abundance everywhere in the world around us. These microorganisms include fungi, bacteria, slime moulds, algae, lichens and viruses. Some are seen only with a microscope; others have visible stages in their life cycles.

Some of these creatures are harmful, causing disease in humans, in other animals and in plants. Most of those which cause disease in humans and other animals are bacteria or viruses. Examples are the bacteria which cause whooping cough and those viruses which cause influenza and the common cold. Other bacteria attack plants, causing diseases such as potato rot. Viruses too may attack plants. Leaf mosaic of tomatoes is a common disease caused by a virus.

Few fungi cause diseases in animals. A fungus which sometimes attacks humans causes athlete's foot. Another example is the fungus which causes ringworm in humans and some animals. Many kinds of fungus attack plants, examples being the downy mildews which we see on the leaves of rose plants, and the fungus which causes silver leaf disease of plum trees.

In Section 1 of the book, you will find out more about each kind of small organism and the part they each play in nature. For safety, you will not be handling those which cause diseases in humans or other animals. In Section 2 you will find out about those small organisms which are specially useful to us. Some of them have been used by humans for many hundreds or thousands of years and continue to play an important part in our way of life today.

Read this before you start

Although most microorganisms are harmless, a few of them can be very harmful and dangerous if they get into the wrong place. This is why the projects in this book deal only with the harmless kinds. Even so, it is sensible to take care that large numbers of harmful organisms cannot get into the wrong place by accident. The instructions in the book are designed to prevent this from happening.

There are a few specially important rules which you should always keep to when you are using this book:

1   When you are working on the topics of Section 1:
Work in a clean room, but preferably not a kitchen. A laboratory, a utility room, or a clean garden shed is a better choice.

Wash your hands every time you finish working, even if you are only breaking off for a few minutes to do something else.
Do not eat or drink anything while you are working.
Never let the organisms which you grow touch your fingers.

2   When you are making food or drinks in Section 2:
Work in a kitchen or other room suitable for the preparation of food.

Make sure that everything you use, including the surface you work on, is absolutely clean.
Wash your hands every time before you start work.
Wash your hands again from time to time, *and again* when you return to work after a break.

Section I

Microorganisms—what they are and what they do

1 Make a model microorganism

One of the problems of studying microorganisms is that many of them are too small to be seen clearly, even with a microscope. The bacteria and the viruses are the smallest of all living things. The viruses are so small that we need the most powerful kind of microscope, an electron microscope, in order to be able to see anything of them at all. It is partly because they are so small and partly because many of them cause diseases that we do not have many projects on bacteria and viruses in this book. The main exceptions are the bacteria which we use in the making of cheese, butter and yoghurt. In this project we try to get some idea of what bacteria and viruses look like by making some large-scale models.

WHAT YOU NEED

Ten or more spheres about 35–40 mm in diameter: you can use old table-tennis balls, or spheres of expanded polystyrene. If you cannot get ready-made polystyrene or wooden spheres, you could make them from a block of expanded polystyrene or balsa wood.
A fine drill if you are using wooden spheres; a candle or gas flame if you are using table tennis balls.
A needle over 40 mm long (you can make one out of stiff wire bent double and twisted); and button thread or other strong thread.
White or cream paint, if the spheres you are using are not white or cream already.
Stiff wire (e.g. 30 amp): ten pieces each about 15 cm long; six pieces 8 cm long.
A sheet each of: stiff white card, about A4 size, for the bacillus; white writing paper for the virus head; white A4 or foolscap paper for the virus sheath.
Quick-drying adhesive (e.g. clear Bostik).
A large cork or pencil rubber 30 mm across (or pieces of expanded polystyrene or wood).
A used ballpoint pen (BIC or similar) or a pencil or wooden stick of about the same size.
Six nails about 40 mm long.

GETTING STARTED

The first model is the simplest to make. It is a model of a kind of bacterium called a *streptococcus*. The bacteria which we call *cocci* have the shape of a sphere. In the streptococci, the bacteria are grouped together in chains, rather like a string of beads. Some kinds of streptococcus are harmful, such as the ones which cause sore throats. Another kind lives in milk, causing it to go sour if it is kept too long. A third kind is very useful to us; it can live in milk and produces a pleasant and slightly sour taste. We use this bacterium, *Streptococcus cremoris*, for making butter and cheeses, as explained in projects 11 and 12.

If you are using wooden spheres, drill a fine hole through the centre of each. If you are using spheres of polystyrene or plasticine, or are using table tennis balls, you simply thread them all on to a length of button thread, using the needle.

Threading the spheres together

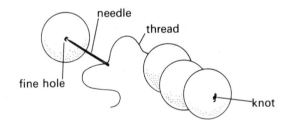

The completed model streptococcus

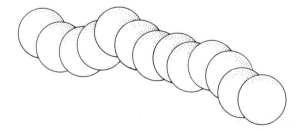

Keep just two of the spheres aside, for making the next model. Tie a knot at each end of the thread to prevent the spheres from slipping off. If the spheres are not already white or cream, paint them. The model streptococcus is now complete.

One way of displaying your model, mounted on an inverted food carton, painted in a contrasting colour.

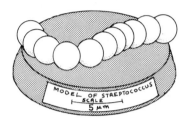

This is supposed to be a scale model, so it is important to work out what its scale is. The diameter of a single individual in a streptococcus chain is about 1 μm. Now, 1 μm (one micrometre) is a millionth of a metre, or a thousandth of a millimetre. If the spheres in your model are 40 mm in diameter, the model is 40 000 times natural size. If your spheres are 35 mm in diameter, the scale of the model is 35 000 times life size.

To get an idea of what this scale means, think of an average 12-year-old boy or girl, who is 1.08 m tall. We choose this age because girls and boys have nearly the same average height then. Magnified 40 000 times, the height is over 40 000 m, or 40 km. This is roughly the distance from Coventry to Leicester, from Glasgow to Stirling, from London to Guildford or from Caernarvon to Llandudno.

The next model is made to the same scale.

WHAT TO DO NEXT

The second model is of a different kind of bacterium, one with a rod-like shape, called a *bacillus*. There are very many kinds of bacilli. Some are long and thin, some shorter and fatter, some with whip-like hairs (*flagella*) as in the model, some without. The hairs are used by the bacillus for moving around in water or in the fluids of the body. Most bacilli are harmless, but some cause diseases. Typhoid and anthrax are examples of diseases caused by bacilli.

Attach the flagella, represented by wires, to each sphere first. If you are using table tennis balls, twist four or more 15 cm wires sufficiently to keep the ends together. Carefully heat the twist at one end over a flame and push the bunch of wires through the ball. After cooling, twist the wires round as in the diagram and glue at one hole, allowing them to protrude about 8 cm at the other. For solid spheres, bore a hole about 10 mm deep in each, fold two or more wires double and push the looped ends into the hole, wedging them with a matchstick if necessary.

Preparing the spheres and the cylinder of paper

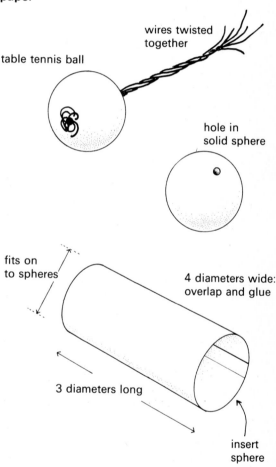

Cut out a rectangle of card and glue it to form a cylinder which fits tightly on to the spheres at each end; the rectangle should be about 3 diameters long by 4 diameters wide, as shown in the drawing. Now glue the spheres into the ends of the cylinder. If the spheres are not white, paint them white now.

3

The completed model bacillus

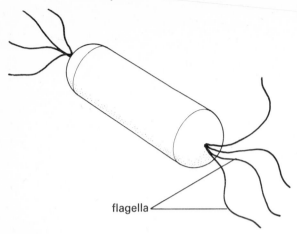

flagella

Bend the wires to suitable shapes as in the drawing to suggest how they lash through the water to make the bacillus move along. The model bacillus is now complete.

The design for the head of the model virus; all dimensions are in millimetres

Trace this outline, cut along the heavy line, fold at the dotted lines and glue the flaps, as shown in the diagram opposite.

A MODEL VIRUS

The virus modelled here is one known as T2. It is a member of a special group of viruses known as the *bacteriophages*. These are viruses which attack bacteria. One of the difficulties in studying viruses is that they can be grown only inside a living organism. If you try to grow them in broth, for example, as used for growing moulds in project 6, they do not multiply. It is not easy to find people who will volunteer to be infected with influenza virus just so that we can study its life history. But we can easily grow large quantities of bacteria and then infect them with bacteriophages, so that we can study these viruses in detail.

T2 has a very complicated structure, more intricate than many of the other known viruses, but one that makes a rather impressive model.

Mark out the design for the head carefully on a sheet of white writing paper. You can trace it from the diagram below. Cut it out and assemble it as shown in the drawings.

The tail may be made from a used ballpoint pen. Make the tail sheath by rolling round the pen a long strip of white paper, marked with thick black lines to represent grooves (see the drawing on page 6).

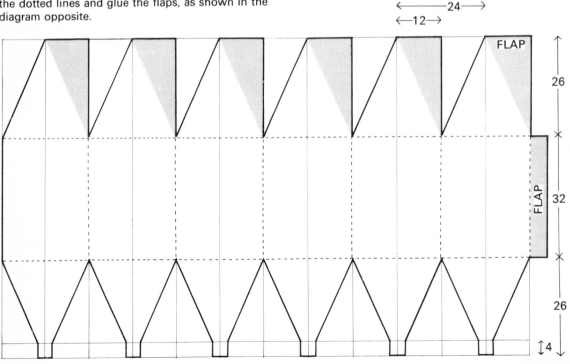

MAKING THE MODEL VIRUS

The head cut out and folded

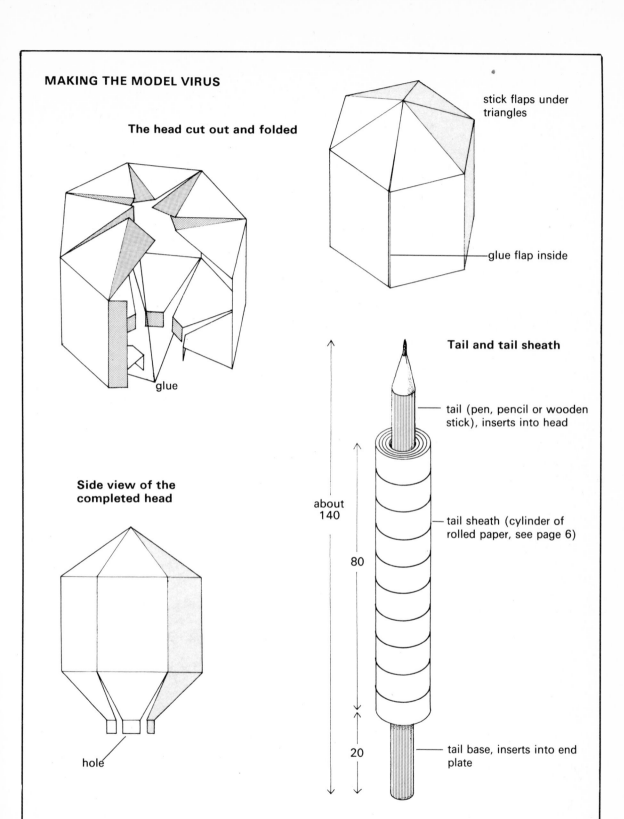

stick flaps under triangles

glue flap inside

glue

Side view of the completed head

hole

about 140

80

20

Tail and tail sheath

tail (pen, pencil or wooden stick), inserts into head

tail sheath (cylinder of rolled paper, see page 6)

tail base, inserts into end plate

Making the tail sheath

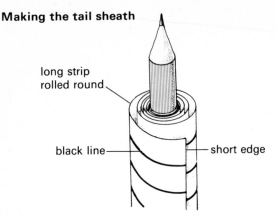

long strip
rolled round

black line ———— short edge

Make a long strip: cut A4 or foolscap sheet into 4 strips across width, join strips end to end—length about 800 mm. Mark thick black lines 50 mm long at one short edge. Stick the other short edge to the tail and roll the paper tightly round, sticking down the lined end.

A cork or thick rubber cut into a hexagonal shape is glued to the end of the tail, forming the end plate. Push six long nails through it at the corners. Bend the six 8-cm lengths of stiff wire as shown, then push them through the upper corners of the hexagonal end plate. Paint the model white if it is not white already.

Since viruses are so much smaller than bacteria, this model is on a much larger scale than the other two. The T2 virus is about 400 nm long.

Assembling the end plate from a large cork or rubber

hole to fit tail

30

head of 40 mm nail

12–15

hole for wire

point of nail

1 nm (one nanometre) is a thousand-millionth of a metre, or a millionth of a millimetre. If your model is 150 mm long, the scale is:

$$\frac{150}{400} = 0.375 \text{ million times} = 375\,000 \text{ times.}$$

The height of an average 12-year-old boy or girl modelled to the same scale would be $1.08 \times 375\,000 = 405\,000$ m $= 405$ km. This is equal to the distance from Coventry to Glasgow, or from Caernarvon to Brighton. Think of this distance, then look at your model and you will begin to realize just how small are the viruses.

You can see the remarkable way the virus structure operates in the diagram of its life cycle.

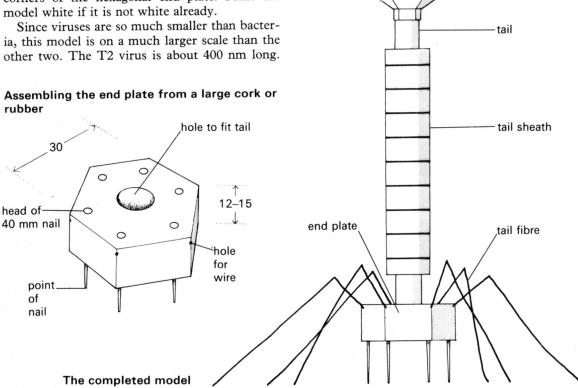

head

tail

tail sheath

end plate

tail fibre

The completed model

THE LIFE STORY OF THE T2 VIRUS

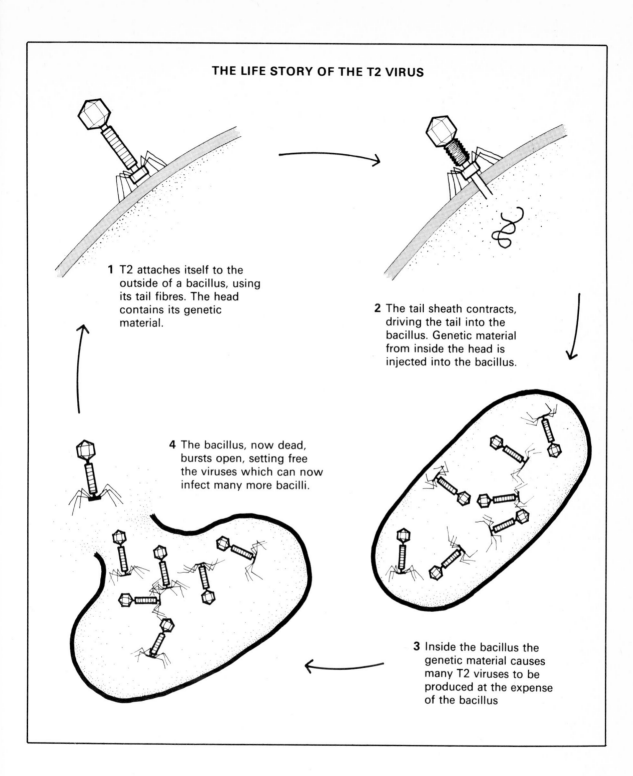

1 T2 attaches itself to the outside of a bacillus, using its tail fibres. The head contains its genetic material.

2 The tail sheath contracts, driving the tail into the bacillus. Genetic material from inside the head is injected into the bacillus.

3 Inside the bacillus the genetic material causes many T2 viruses to be produced at the expense of the bacillus

4 The bacillus, now dead, bursts open, setting free the viruses which can now infect many more bacilli.

2 The attackers

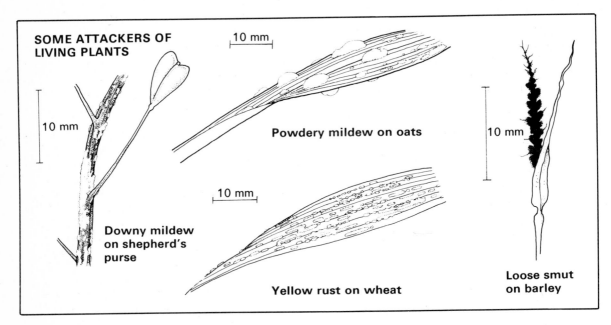

SOME ATTACKERS OF LIVING PLANTS

10 mm

10 mm

Powdery mildew on oats

Downy mildew on shepherd's purse

10 mm

10 mm

Yellow rust on wheat

Loose smut on barley

Many small organisms attack living plants and animals by living in their bodies and feeding on them. They usually cause the plant or animal to become diseased. We shall not try to have adventures with those which cause diseases in animals—this could be unpleasant and dangerous.

The microorganisms which attack plants can be divided into three groups, the *viruses*, the *bacteria* and the *fungi*. Viruses cause diseases such as tomato mosaic, in which the leaves of tomato plants become yellowish in patches, so that the leaf looks like a mosaic. The plant grows poorly, produces few fruits and may die. Although the effects of the disease are easy to see, viruses themselves are the smallest of all living things and cannot be seen, except with an electron microscope. Bacteria cause diseases such as canker on plum and cherry trees and diseases in which the living stems and buds of potato and rhubarb rot away. The effects of the attack can be serious and are often incurable. Bacteria are so small that they appear only as tiny specks under a high-powered microscope, so they are not particularly interesting to look at.

Fungi are larger than viruses and bacteria. They can be seen with a low-powered microscope or hand lens and some can even be seen with the unaided eye. This makes them very good subjects for an adventure. Although very few indeed attack animals, there are many different kinds of fungus which attack plants. This means that they are easy to find and much safer to work with.

Fungi are the cause of several important and devastating diseases of crop plants. Perhaps the most serious is Potato Blight, caused by the fungus *Phytophthora infestans*. This fungus was responsible for the devastating Potato Famine in Ireland in the nineteenth century, and it is still a problem today.

A plant which is being attacked by a fungus is called the *host* plant. The fungus lives inside the living host and feeds destructively on the tissues of the host. For this reason the fungus is called a *parasite*.

Not only do fungi attack crop plants but they are parasites on many garden plants and wild plants too. You will not have to look far to find some to study.

WHAT YOU NEED

Pair of fine-pointed scissors for collecting diseased parts of plants.

Small bottles, plastic cartons or similar small containers for holding the material you collect.

Packet of self-adhesive labels, small size (e.g. 1 cm × 3 cm).

A hand lens.

Mounted needle (two needles, if possible) for handling the fungus.

Some microscope slides and cover slips, or small glass or clear plastic sheets.

Squeeze-pipette (eye-dropper) for putting water on the slides.

A microscope. Though not essential, it is a great help for looking at the smaller fungi. It need not be a powerful one. A magnification of ×40 is quite enough, although ×100 will help you to see more.

Razor blade.

Small flower pot or saucer. Glass or plastic tumbler.

Packet of cress seeds.

GETTING STARTED

The fungus enters a plant and grows inside its host, and for some time no signs are visible from the outside. Later the fungus produces spores by means of which it can spread to other hosts. Most fungi rely on the air to carry their spores, so the spores are produced on the outside of the host.

The drawings show various ways in which fungi arrange for their spores to catch the wind. It is at this stage that it becomes obvious that the host is being attacked. The visible stage is reached when the fungus has had time to mature, usually from May onwards, so that May is the best month to begin this project.

The table on page 11, and the drawings, will help you to recognize the signs of attack by fungi. There are several major groups of fungal parasite, and you will soon learn the main features of each group.

When possible, it is a good idea to begin in the garden. Most gardening books have chapters on plant diseases, some with colour photographs of diseased plants. If you can borrow such a book, you will have no difficulty in finding and identifying material.

If you live in a town, it is usually easy to find weed plants such as shepherd's purse growing in cracks in the pavement. Snapdragons are now and then found growing on old brick walls. Michaelmas daisies are another kind to look for. These are frequently attacked by fungi (see table, p. 11). There are many others to be found if you look in out-of-the-way places.

Having found a plant which is obviously diseased, cut off the diseased part and put it in one of the small containers. Label the container with the name of the plant and the place in which it was found. In the case of fungi such as the bracket fungi, which have very large sporing bodies, you can simply cut out a piece of this for study.

How spores are released into the air to be carried away by currents

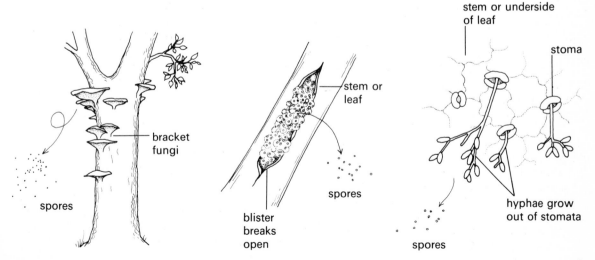

9

WHAT TO DO NEXT

Look at the diseased part under a lens. Is the surface of the plant broken or blistered, so that the spores are easily visible from the outside? Can you see thin cotton-wool-like threads (hyphae) of the fungus on the outside of the plant?

If the fungus is not completely inside the plant, use the needle to remove some of it for study. Place a drop of water on a microscope slide (or on a small sheet of glass or transparent plastic) and place the piece of fungus in the drop. You can hold this up to a light and look at it with a lens. If you have a microscope, cover the drop with a cover slip before examining it under the microscope.

Look for spores. What colour are they? What shape are they? How many are there? Are they produced singly, in chains, on branching tufts of hyphae? Or are they arranged in some other way? Make a few sketches to show what you see.

How to hold a stem and cut a section using a razor blade

material to cut. Cut the stem across where there is a patch of disease. Wet the cut end and the razor blade, then slice across, cutting sections about half a millimetre thick. There is little point in trying to cut them any thinner. Transfer a section to a drop of water on a microscope slide and examine as described above. You will not find it easy to pick out the hyphae which are woven in and around the cells of the stem but it should be easy to see regions where spores are forming.

Spores on a brush-like structure

Spores on branched hyphae

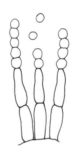

Spores in chains

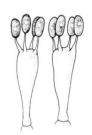

Spores in groups of four, as in bracket fungi and most other of the larger fungi

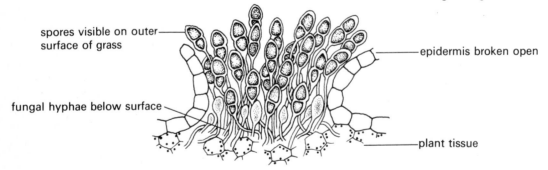

spores visible on outer surface of grass

epidermis broken open

fungal hyphae below surface

plant tissue

Section through a 'blister' on the blade of a grass, caused by a rust fungus

If the fungus is not visible on the surface of the plant you will need to cut sections of the plant to see the fungus properly. Stems are the easiest

The larger spore-forming bodies can be cut in thin sections as described above, and examined for spores.

SOME THINGS TO TRY

Seedlings grown close together under very damp conditions, such as in boxes of compost, often suffer from the disease called 'damping off'. The stem of the seedling becomes soft and thin just where it leaves the soil. The top of the seedling falls over and eventually the seedling dies.

Try growing some cress seedlings under conditions which help the damping-off fungus (*Pythium*) to attack the plant. Sow the seeds very thickly on soil in a pot or a saucer. Cover with a glass tumbler to keep conditions really moist. Water often. After the seeds have begun to grow you should find some of them falling over. Cut out pieces of the stem at soil level and mount them as described above. Look for spores. If these are not easily seen, pull (or tease) the diseased stem apart using two needles. It is soft

Cress seedlings

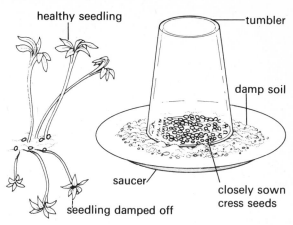

and the cells will separate easily. Put a cover slip on the teased stem. Slight pressure on the cover

SOME FUNGI WHICH ATTACK LIVING PLANTS

Name of fungus or group	Examples of plants attacked	Part attacked	Appearance of disease
Rusts	Snapdragon, hollyhock, chrysanthemum, rose, groundsel, plum, currant, grasses and cereals	Leaves	Yellow, brown, or orange patches, looking like rusty spots
Smuts	Grasses and cereals	Leaves and flowers	Blackish patches, like sooty smuts
Pythium (damping off)	Young seedlings of many kinds of plant	Stem at soil level	Stem goes soft
Downy mildews	Wallflower, snapdragon, clover, shepherd's purse, cauliflower, lettuce, onion	Leaves and stems	Whitish patches like cotton wool
Powdery mildews	Apple, pea, marrow, currant, rose, many garden flower plants, grasses and cereals, oak	Leaves and stems	Powdery patches (spores); later, tiny black dots (sexual spores)
Botrytis (grey mould)	Many kinds of plant, both in gardens and in the wild	Leaves, stems, flowers and fruits	Grey cotton-wool-like patches
Blight	Potato	Leaves, stems and tubers	Brown patches, becoming black and wet
Bracket fungi	Tree trunk	Trunk	See drawing, p. 9

slip will help to spread out the material, making the spores and the hyphae easier to see.

How do spores get to the seedlings to cause the disease? Do they come from the soil? Try the same experiment, but use soil which has first been baked in an oven for 30 minutes, then cooled and moistened with tap water. Do the seedlings become damped off now?

Can damping off be prevented by treatment? To test this, try growing the seedlings on fresh garden soil, as before, but sow them thinly and do not cover them with the tumbler. This gives drier conditions. Does *Pythium* attack the plant under these conditions and if so, is the attack as severe as in the covered seedlings?

Also try growing seeds under damp crowded conditions (as you did at first), but treat the seeds or the soil with a fungicide. Several kinds can be bought in a garden shop; it is important that you follow the directions which are provided with the packet. Is the fungicide effective in preventing the disease?

How do the spores get carried from an infected plant to one which is not infected? Does the water help carry them? Grow two sets of seedlings, one in dry conditions, the other in damp conditions. When the seedlings in damp conditions begin to damp off, drain some of the water from their pot into the other pot. Does this action transfer the disease to the other pot?

3 The decomposers

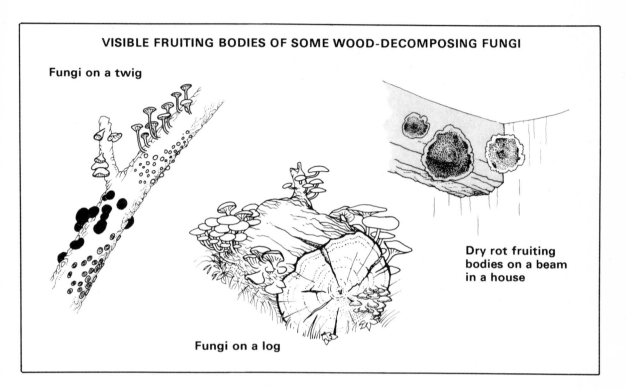

VISIBLE FRUITING BODIES OF SOME WOOD-DECOMPOSING FUNGI

Fungi on a twig

Fungi on a log

Dry rot fruiting bodies on a beam in a house

In project 2 you looked at some of the very small living things which attack other living things. These parasites generally cause harm to the creatures they attack. The *decomposers* are living things which feed on the dead bodies of other living things. They rot them away gradually, until nothing is left except for parts such as bones and shells which cannot be decomposed.

Yeast is a decomposer. It feeds on the sugars from crushed grapes or on solutions of sugar which we provide for it when making wine, bread or beer. Yeast is a useful decomposer, and so are several more which we shall meet in later chapters. We regard many other decomposers as dangerous. Examples are the dry rot fungus which attacks and destroys the wooden parts of buildings, and the many fungi and bacteria which spoil our food if we keep it too long.

The decomposers play a very important part in nature. If it were not for these organisms, the Earth would be covered with a deep layer of dead leaves, fallen trees, dead plants and the bodies of dead animals. The layer would not increase in thickness for ever, since after a while no more plants would grow. The reason is that plants need a continuous supply of mineral salts from the soil.

While the plant is alive the minerals it has taken from the soil are held in its body. When it dies and is rotted away by the decomposers, these minerals are returned to the soil again for use by the newly growing plants. The decomposers are responsible for recycling the minerals which are so essential to the growth of plants. Animals need minerals and organic materials too, and get them by feeding on plants or other animals. So animals too depend on decomposers to recycle the minerals.

Decomposers may be fungi (which include the yeasts) or bacteria. In this project we see what some of them look like.

WHAT YOU NEED

Plastic dishes or some old china saucers. Dishes can be made by cutting the bottoms from plastic bottles and food containers.
A supply of paper tissues.
A roll of food-wrapping film (Clingfilm, Gladwrap, etc.).
A small amount of powdered calcium carbonate.
A small packet of general garden fertilizer (Chempak or Phostrogen).

GETTING STARTED

The aim is to grow some of the fungi which decompose our food. Prepare some dishes containing various foods such as bread, sliced turnip, sliced potato, sliced onion and cottage cheese but *not* meat. First of all, line the dish with a double layer of paper tissue. Soak the paper with water, then pour off the surplus water. The damp paper helps to keep conditions in the dish moist, but not too moist. The slices of food or layer of cottage cheese need not be more than 5 mm thick.

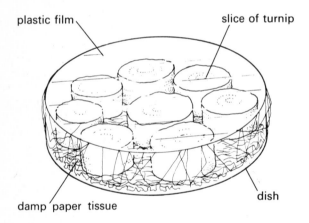

plastic film

slice of turnip

damp paper tissue

dish

Growing decomposers on food

Make sure that there will be space above the food when the dish is covered. Stretch a piece of food wrapping film across the top of the dish and press it down around the sides which should be dry. The film should be stretched as tightly as possible, so that you can see clearly into the dish. You may find that the film does not stick firmly to certain kinds of plastic. In this event, seal the film to the dish with sticky tape.

It is interesting to prepare several dishes with the same kinds of food and to put these in different places. Here are some places to try:

A cool place: in a deep-freezer; it is not a good idea to put the dish in an ordinary refrigerator, for the food stored there may become contaminated. In winter, you could put the dish in a shed or garage outdoors.
A warm place: in an airing cupboard.
A light place: on a window-sill in a living room.
A dark place: in a cupboard in a living room.

You could also try soaking the bread in vinegar before putting it in the dish. Vinegar is an acid and some decomposers do not like acid conditions. On the other hand some prefer acid conditions, so the vinegared bread could have quite a number of interesting things growing on it.

Look at the dishes every day, using a lens. It is best not to remove the film. If the inner surface of the film becomes cloudy with drops of water, shake the dish a little to make the small drops join together to make bigger drops. Then tilt the dish and the big drops will run back into the dish.

Most of the decomposers which you will see are fungi. You will first see a tuft of cotton-wool-like threads (the hyphae), which are white or greyish. Sometimes the hyphae are quite thick and wiry and spread rapidly over the whole of the food. Other fungi spread more slowly forming roughly circular patches. These will soon bear spores, often coloured greenish-blue, various other shades of green or other colours, including grey and black.

It is very important not to open the dish, for some people are affected if they breathe in large numbers of spores in the air. On some of the fungi you will be able to see the tiny sporangia in which the spores are produced. The pin-mould is a common decomposer. Its sporangia look like tiny pins sticking into the food. The 'head' of the pin is the sporangium which later bursts to release hundreds of spores. Some kinds of pin-mould produce their sporangia singly, while others produce them in tufts (see drawings, p. 15).

There will probably be several yeasts growing on the food. Some of these may be ordinary brewer's or baker's yeast but they are more likely to be wild yeasts of various kinds. They do not have hyphae but grow as a slimy shiny patch which may be white or cream in colour or even pink or red. Cooked rice and similar foods which

14

Typical mould fungus growing on food

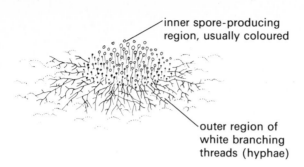

inner spore-producing region, usually coloured

outer region of white branching threads (hyphae)

Two kinds of pin-mould

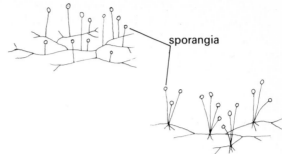

sporangia

have been kept too long may show pink or red patches, usually caused by yeasts growing on them.

After a week or so the food will probably be completely covered with fungi and decomposition will be well under way. At this stage you are not likely to see any new decomposers on the food. Dispose of the dishes without removing the film. Put them in a large polythene bag; seal the bag with a wire 'tie' and put the bag in the refuse bin.

DECOMPOSING CELLULOSE

Plant tissues consist of cells. Each cell is enclosed in a cell wall. Cell walls are made mainly of cellulose. This substance is not easy to decompose, and there are few decomposers which can feed on it. Yet, since this material is one of the main solid materials present in plants, the decomposition of cellulose is an essential part of the natural cycle of decay. This investigation is similar to the one you have just done with foods. Here the 'food' is paper tissue. Paper comes from plants and consists mainly of cellulose, so cellulose decomposers will grow well on it. They need mineral salts in addition which we can provide as a solution of garden fertilizer.

Set up two or three dishes just like those in the previous project, but put a layer of shredded white paper tissue into the dish, with no other food. Sprinkle a small pinch of calcium carbonate (chalk, but *not* blackboard chalk, which is not calcium carbonate) over the paper in each dish as this creates the right conditions for the

decomposers. Make up a solution (about 100 cm³) of chemical fertilizer, such as Phostrogen or one of the Chempak liquid fertilizers. Read the directions on the packet, but make it up with 4 times the recommended amount of water, to give quarter-strength solution. Pour this solution into the dish to soak the paper. Then pour away the surplus, leaving the paper damp but not submerged.

Take a teaspoonful of garden soil and put it in a tumbler half filled with water. Stir vigorously for several minutes. This makes a suspension of soil organisms. It is to be hoped that among them will be the spores of fungi which can decompose cellulose. This step is necessary because it is unlikely that you will find many cellulose decomposers already on the paper or in your home. Add half a teaspoonful of the suspension to each dish.

Instead of the soil suspension, you can add small crumbled pieces of rotting wood or bark. This will be rich in cellulose decomposers which will spread from the wood or bark and begin to grow on the paper.

Cover the dishes with food film, as before, label them 'Cellulose' and put them where they will be at a steady and moderate temperature. A cupboard in a living room is most suitable. Cellulose decomposers do not usually grow quickly, so it may be several weeks before anything definite is seen. Look at the dishes once a week. Some of the decomposers produce coloured substances, so look for black or coloured patches on the paper. Since no other kind of organic food material such as sugar or starch has been provided in the dishes, you can be certain that anything that grows there is capable of using cellulose as its food.

4 Moulds in the soil

The soil is teeming with many kinds of extremely small organisms. Most of these are what we have described as the decomposers (project 3, p. 13), but there are plenty of attackers too (project 2, p. 8). The decomposers soon get to work on any dead matter, rotting it down, and assisting in the return of its mineral salts to the soil.

The following investigation shows how, in nature, decomposers are encouraged to grow when they are provided with a suitable material to grow on. The material in this investigation is the rather jelly-like material which surrounds cress seeds when they are soaked in water. It is the food of several different fungi and, being easy to handle on a microscope slide, it gives us a chance to see what the decomposers really look like in their natural surroundings.

WHAT YOU NEED

A kettle and a small saucepan.
Tablespoon and teaspoon.
Baking tray and aluminium kitchen foil to line it.
A cupful of garden soil.

A few (20–30) cress seeds.
Bottle of Milton.
Glass jug or china basin to hold about 1 litre.
Five plastic dishes with lids. You can use old china saucers with food film (Clingfilm, Glad-wrap, etc.) stretched across the top. Small plastic or glass bottles with caps, or stoppered test-tubes can be used also.
Pair of forceps (tweezers).
Hand lens (× 8 or × 10).
A microscope: a simple one with magnification of × 20 is good enough.
Microscope slides (plain or cavity).

GETTING STARTED

Boil a few cupfuls of water. Leave it in the kettle to cool.

Spread 2 or 3 tablespoonfuls of fresh garden soil on to a metal baking tray and heat it in an oven set to 140°C (275°F, Gas mark 1) for 20 minutes. It is a good idea to line the tray with aluminium kitchen foil. Put the cress seeds into the saucepan and half fill the pan with water.

Containers suitable for this investigation

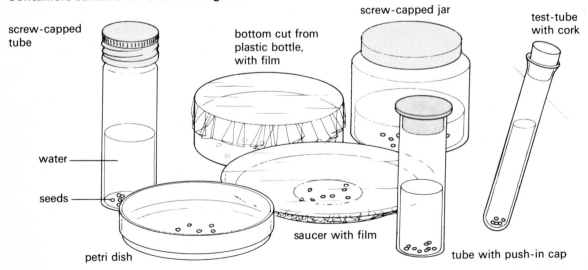

screw-capped tube

bottom cut from plastic bottle, with film

screw-capped jar

test-tube with cork

water

seeds

petri dish

saucer with film

tube with push-in cap

16

Bring it to the boil and let it simmer for 20 minutes. This kills the seeds. It also sterilizes them so that no living spores are on them.

While the seeds are simmering, make up 1 litre of Milton solution according to the instructions on the bottle. The usual mixture is 2 capfuls to 1 litre of cold water. Wipe the area of the table on which you are working with a paper tissue soaked in the Milton solution. Fill four of the dishes (or tubes) with solution. Put their lids or caps into the jug or bowl, together with the forceps, so that they are covered with solution. The Milton is being used to kill any small creatures or spores which might already be in or on the equipment. Leave each item soaking for 10 minutes, then rinse it under a cold running tap. Place it upside down to drain, and to reduce the chance of spores settling in it while it is standing. Although tap water *could* contain some organisms, these are likely to be very few, and probably none which will grow on the seeds.

Once the seeds are boiled and the soil is baked, you are ready to set up the dishes. Label the dishes as you treat them:

Dish 1, Boiled Water. Partly fill the dish with boiled cooled water. Add 5 boiled cress seeds, using the forceps. Cover the dish. This tests whether boiling kills fungi and their spores.

Dish 2, Baked Soil. Partly fill the dish with boiled cooled water. Add a half a teaspoonful of baked soil and 5 boiled cress seeds. Cover the dish. This tests whether baking kills fungi or their spores and whether the soil itself (rather than the living things in it) is responsible for decomposing.

Dish 3, Fresh Soil. As Dish 2, but use fresh (unbaked) garden soil. This should provide a rich supply of decomposers.

Put all the dishes together in a warm room. Carry them carefully so they do not spill, and put them where they will not be disturbed.

WHAT TO DO NEXT

By the next day the layer around the seeds will have swollen and become quite jelly-like. You may not be able to see it easily, but you will realize that it is there when you try to pick up the seeds with the forceps!

Boil a cupful or two of water in the kettle and leave it in the kettle to cool. Make up another jugful of Milton solution. Wipe down your working area with some of this solution. Sterilize the two remaining dishes and the forceps in Milton, as you did yesterday.

Now transfer the seeds from Dish 2 to one of the new dishes. Cover it and label this new dish 'Dish 2'. Wash out the original Dish 2, which is no longer needed. Similarly, transfer the seeds from Dish 3 to the remaining dish, calling this 'Dish 3'. Put the new dishes with Dish 1.

Examine the dishes every day, using a hand lens. Does *anything* grow on the seeds in Dishes 1 or 2? When you see any signs of growth in any of these dishes or dish 3, transfer some of the seeds to a microscope slide to look at them more closely. (Afterwards, they can be put back into the dishes for a few more days to allow further growth to occur.) Put plenty of water on the slide. If you have a cavity slide, use this, for the seed can then be surrounded with plenty of water. The fungi float clear of the seed and can be seen more clearly. After a few days, you may be able to see spores forming as shown on p. 10.

5 The slime moulds

These are a group of living things which are quite common yet we hardly ever notice them. Although 'moulds' suggest that they are a kind of fungus, they are members of a distinct and rather separate group.

They certainly have unusual features in their life history, as the drawings show. At one stage a slime mould consists of many small cells, looking rather like the single-celled animal *Amoeba*, but much smaller in size. These amoebae move around, feeding on bacteria in the soil or wherever else they are living. They feed, grow and then reproduce by splitting into two.

When the food supply begins to run out they move towards each other and fuse to make a *plasmodium*. This has many nuclei in it, one from each of the amoebae which fused together. The plasmodium is often brightly coloured and is easily seen under a lens. It may then form a *sclerotium*, which is a dry object containing

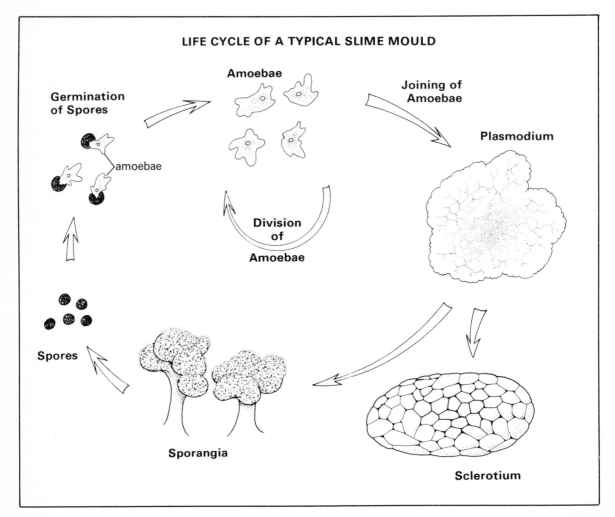

LIFE CYCLE OF A TYPICAL SLIME MOULD

Germination of Spores

Amoebae

amoebae

Joining of Amoebae

Plasmodium

Division of Amoebae

Spores

Sporangia

Sclerotium

many spores. Or the plasmodium may send up a stalk forming a *sporangium* at the end of it. The sporangium also contains many *spores*.

The spores can be carried away from the sporangium in the air, or by splashing drops of rain. They are able to withstand unfavourable conditions, such as drying out of the soil. When conditions are favourable, such as when there are

A grex producing a sporangium

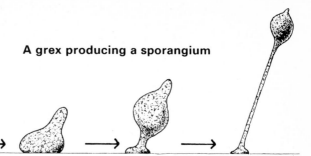

GREX

plenty of bacteria for food, each spore gives rise to a single amoeba. The amoebae feed and grow, so completing the life cycle.

One type of slime mould does not form a plasmodium. The amoebae come together, but do not fuse. This becomes a many-celled creature called a *grex*. The grex is shaped rather like a slug, but it is much smaller and simpler in structure. It creeps along and eventually sends up a stalk with a sporangium on the end of it.

Slime moulds live where bacteria are plentiful, especially in the soil, on rotting plant matter and on dead logs. In this chapter we will try to grow some of the slime moulds found on the bark of trees.

WHAT YOU NEED

A scalpel or sharp knife.
Several shallow dishes of transparent plastic with covers. The best are the plastic petri dishes used for growing bacteria. If these are not available, you can make something suitable from food containers of various kinds, as p. 16. Use clear covers, e.g. transparent cartons or food film.

A supply of white paper tissues.
Scissors.
Small adhesive labels.
A hand lens, × 10 if possible.
A squeeze-pipette (eye-dropper).

GETTING STARTED

The best time for this project is autumn, but you can try it at other times of the year too. Use the bark of almost any kind of tree, but oak, ash and sycamore are good ones to begin with.

Using the scalpel or sharp knife, peel *thin* strips of bark from the tree. In doing this you must never cut deeply into the bark, for this will damage it and help disease-causing bacteria and fungi attack the tree. It is best if you take the bark from trunks or branches of trees which have already been felled. Logs sold as firewood often have bark which is rich in slime moulds, especially if the wood has been allowed to become damp and the bark is beginning to rot. Some trees (e.g. lilac, holly) have flaky bark and you can strip off small pieces without damaging the tree.

If possible, collect bark from several different kinds of tree. Note which tree each sample comes from, so you will know which trees were the best sources of slime moulds.

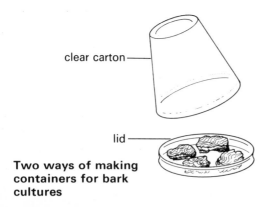

clear carton

lid

Two ways of making containers for bark cultures

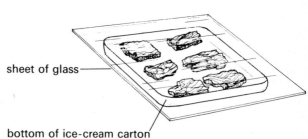

sheet of glass

bottom of ice-cream carton cut to 1 cm high

Wash out the dishes with warm water, then rinse them in cold water and let them drain. You need a supply of boiled water for soaking the bark. Boil a litre of water in a saucepan for several minutes, then pour it into a heat-resistant jug and let it cool.

Cut pieces of paper tissue to fit the bottom of your dishes. Pour a little cooled boiled water into each dish and arrange the pieces of bark in the dish. The original surface of each piece should face upward. The water should just cover the bark so that it is able to become fully soaked.

Label the dishes with the types of bark they contain and put them away until the following day.

WHAT TO DO NEXT

By the next day the bark should have soaked up plenty of water. Pour off the rest of the water, leaving the paper tissue slightly damp. Put the covers on the dishes again and place the dishes on a window sill. Many slime moulds do not produce sporangia unless they have light. Yet they must not have strong sunlight, so choose a window sill which is shaded from direct sunlight.

A bark culture opened for examination

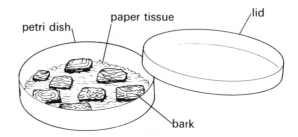

petri dish · paper tissue · lid · bark

Look at the pieces of bark every day, using the lens. Hold the lens close to your eye, then bring the dish up towards the lens until you can see the surface of the bark sharply focused. In this way you will obtain the maximum magnification.

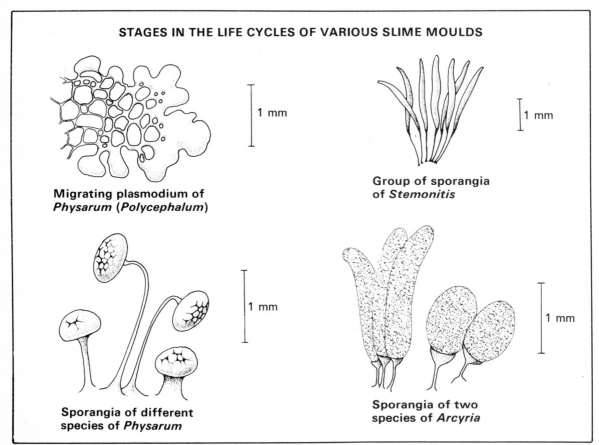

STAGES IN THE LIFE CYCLES OF VARIOUS SLIME MOULDS

Migrating plasmodium of *Physarum (Polycephalum)* — 1 mm

Group of sporangia of *Stemonitis* — 1 mm

Sporangia of different species of *Physarum* — 1 mm

Sporangia of two species of *Arcyria* — 1 mm

Look for brightly coloured or white slimy patches on the bark. They may be only a millimetre or two across, though they can be bigger. These are plasmodia. It may be several days or even a week or two before anything like this is seen, so be patient.

Watch the plasmodia carefully. Look at them several times during a period of an hour or more. Do they move? Do they move off the bark on to the paper tissue? Do they move towards the light, away from it, or are they not affected by the direction of light?

After a few more days you may see a plasmodium producing a sporangium. If you have some of the cellular slime-moulds in your culture you will see the rather slug-shaped body of a grex. This is about 3 mm long. This too may produce a sporangium. Does the grex move towards light or away from it?

You may need to keep the bark cultures going for several weeks. Make sure that they never dry out by adding a drop or two of the boiled water from time to time. Keep the bark and paper moist but not soaked.

The bark may have other small living things on it. You may see patches of algae (which are green and do not move), mosses, lichens (project 13) and the hyphae of various rotting fungi (project 3). These plants and the fungi are food for many kinds of small animals which spend their life on the bark, such as collembola (springtails), millepedes and many kinds of small beetle. Some of these may have found their way in to the bark cultures and provide additional interest.

6 Moulds in the air

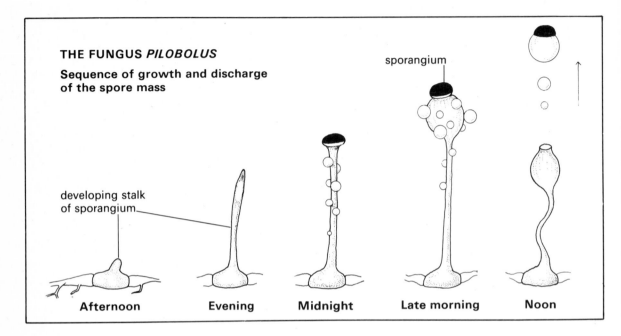

THE FUNGUS *PILOBOLUS*

Sequence of growth and discharge of the spore mass

developing stalk of sporangium

sporangium

Afternoon   Evening   Midnight   Late morning   Noon

Several times in this book it has been mentioned that fungi reproduce by means of spores. These spores are carried on air currents away from the fungus which made them to some other place where, if conditions are favourable, they will be able to grow.

There are several ways in which the spores are spread. A few fungi are able to shoot their spores out at high speed, in a jet. The spores may be shot a distance of up to 8 metres. Some make use of insects, which crawl over rotting material, feeding on it and picking up fungal spores on their legs and body. Then they crawl away or fly away, leaving a trail of spores wherever they go. The spores of some fungi are dispersed by rain. The splashing raindrops carry the spores for distances of several centimetres. As we have seen in other chapters, many fungi discharge their spores into the air. Spores are so light that they remain suspended in even the slightest of air currents. They can be carried away for kilometres before they eventually land. It seems hard to believe that the air in the room we are in contains several thousand spores. This investigation sets out to find out if this is so.

WHAT YOU NEED

A small saucepan.
Enough dried soup powder to make about 150 cm³ of soup. You can buy a larger packet, use part and eat the rest. Choose a vegetable soup or consommé, without too many vegetables or pieces of meat in it. Do not use strongly tasting soups such as tomato soup.
Fine kitchen sieve.
A jug or basin, capacity about 500 cm³.
Bottle of Milton.
Six small glass or plastic tubes or bottles, with caps. If you use plastic tubes, they must be able to hold boiling liquid without going out of shape.
A heatproof support, such as an old china cup or small saucepan, to steady the tubes while pouring.
A plastic funnel with a stem narrow enough to fit loosely into the tubes.
Small adhesive labels.

GETTING STARTED

This project uses tubes containing soup, as suitable places in which spores can begin to grow. In a saucepan, mix enough water and soup powder to make about 150 cm³, following the instructions of the packet. When the soup has boiled and the pieces of vegetable (if any) are swollen, pour the soup through the sieve into the basin or jug. Throw away the vegetables and return the soup to the saucepan. Keep the soup simmering gently for 20 minutes, but make sure it does not boil dry. This is to sterilize it. Wash out the basin.

While the soup is simmering, make up about 600 cm³ of Milton solution in the jug or basin. Use a paper tissue soaked in Milton solution to wipe down the area of the table on which you are working. Pour some of the solution through the funnel several times to sterilize it. Then rinse the funnel in cold running water. Leave it upside down on the table to drain. Fill all the tubes with Milton solution. Put the caps in the basin so that they are covered with solution. After 10 minutes, rinse the tubes under a cold running tap, turn

the tubes about in a sink or large bowl filled with cold water. In a minute or two the soup should be at room temperature. Note the time and stand the tubes on the table, still without their caps.

Ten minutes later, put the caps loosely on two of the tubes. Label these tubes '10'. After an hour, cap the remaining tubes loosely and label them '60'. You now have a series of tubes, two of each kind, that has been exposed to the air for 0, 10 and 60 minutes. Put the tubes in a warm place (e.g. a living room near the fireplace or in an airing cupboard) and wait to see what grows in them. Look at them every day for a week or two: without removing the caps, look for signs of fungi growing in or on the soup.

Open the tubes one at a time with great care so as not to splash the soup around. Add strong household disinfectant to the solution in each tube, filling it to the top. Put the caps on again, screwing them down tightly and shake the tube gently. Leave the tubes to stand for 24 hours. They can then be opened and the contents washed away down the sink. Wash the tubes thoroughly. Finally, wash your hands.

The investigation in progress

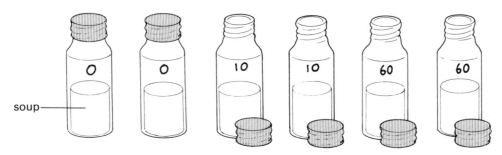

soup

them upside down and stand them on the table to drain. Rinse the caps and drain these too.

When the soup has been simmering for 20 minutes, turn up the heat slightly to bring it fully to the boil. Stand two of the tubes upright in a cup. Pour soup into them through a funnel to a depth of about 2 cm. Immediately put the caps on the tubes but do not screw them on tightly. Label these tubes '0', to show that they have had no exposure to the air. It is to be hoped that if any spores have been able to get into these tubes, they will have been killed by the heat.

Pour equal quantities of soup into the other four tubes, but do not put the caps on yet. Swirl

SOME OTHER THINGS TO TRY

You can use this method to compare the air in different places, to find out where spores occur in greatest numbers. Try exposing tubes in different places and under different conditions, such as:

Different rooms in your house.
Indoors and outdoors.
Outdoors on a still day and outdoors on a windy day.
Near a haystack or in a farmyard.
In a cellar.
In a country area and in a city area.

Section 2

How microorganisms help us

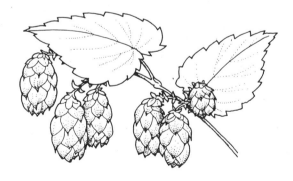

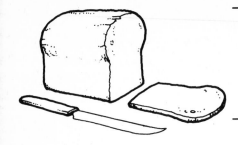

7 Making bread

People have used yeast for making bread for thousands of years. It is probably the most common way in which we make use of extremely small living creatures. The main ingredient of bread is flour. We mix it with water to make dough. Dough baked just as it is, is called 'unleavened' bread. The word 'unleavened' means that there is nothing in the dough to make it rise. The bread is rather solid in texture, quite unlike the bread we normally eat. We can leaven the bread by mixing chemicals (for example, baking powder) into the dough. These chemicals produce millions of tiny bubbles of carbon dioxide gas inside the dough when it is baked. Heating also expands the bubbles, giving the bread its light airy texture.

Although baking powder may be used for making cakes, normally we use living yeast for leavening. Initially, yeast is able to use sugar but not flour as a food, so the yeast is first mixed with a small amount of sugar in water. This mixture is added to the flour, forming a dough which

WHAT YOU NEED

Equipment

- *A bread tin, about 10 cm wide × 20 cm long × 10 cm high. It is worth buying one if you intend to make bread several times. If not, make one from aluminium kitchen foil as described below. For this you need a sheet 45 cm wide (the standard 'wide' foil) and 36 cm long.*
- *Use of an oven and kitchen scales, pastry board (or clean plastic-topped table), wire cooling rack (optional) and a warm kitchen.*
- *A large jug for water, and a small jug, bowl or mug for mixing the yeast.*
- *A teaspoon, a dessertspoon and a mixing spoon.*
- *A clean cloth, such as a tea-towel.*
- *A cup for dusting flour.*
- *A mixing bowl.*
- *Salt, 1 level dessertspoonful.*
- *A baking tray, or some other metal tray which will fit into the oven.*

Ingredients

- *400 cm³ litres warm water (blood heat).*
- *1 teaspoonful of sugar.*
- *10 g dried yeast (usually packed in 20 g sachets), or 20 g fresh yeast.*
- *0.75 kg wholemeal flour (stone-ground flour is best). This is half of the usual 'large bag'; you can use a whole bag and make two loaves, but make sure your bowl is big enough.*
- *1 dessertspoonful of cooking oil.*
- *A little margarine (preferably the 'soft' kind).*

is well kneaded to mix plenty of air with it, providing oxygen that yeast also needs. Next, the dough is put into a warm place to rise. The yeast uses the sugar as food and produces carbon dioxide while doing so. (In the same way, we breathe in air containing oxygen, use the oxygen in respiration, and give off waste carbon dioxide when we breathe out.) When the dough has risen it contains millions of bubbles of carbon dioxide. The dough is then baked, when it becomes drier and firmer, and the bubbles expand in the heat, giving the bread its fluffy texture.

GETTING STARTED

The first thing is to prepare the yeast, to make it active. Pour about one-third of the water into the small bowl and add the sugar. The water should be warm (about blood temperature, not hotter).

Mixing the yeast mixture and flour

Stir until the sugar is dissolved. Then pour in the yeast and stir to mix well. Cover the bowl with the cloth and put it in a warm place (a warm corner of the kitchen, or an airing cupboard). Leave it for 10–15 minutes. In this time the yeast should begin to break down the sugar and a thick creamy foam will appear on top of the mixture. The yeast is then ready for use.

WHAT TO DO NEXT

Having washed your hands very thoroughly, half-fill the cup with flour and keep this for sprinkling on the table and dusting your hands.

Put the rest of the flour into the mixing bowl and add the salt. The salt is not essential, but is added to improve the taste of the bread. Mix the flour and salt, then make a well in the centre of the flour. Pour the yeast mixture into this well. Stir gently with the mixing spoon for a minute or two. Add the oil and stir a few more times.

The next stage is one that needs some judgement on your part. Stir the dough (you can use a kitchen mixer with a dough-hook, if you prefer) and add the rest of the warm water *a little at a time.*

Stir several times each time you add water. *You may not need to add all of the water.* The mixture is crumbly at first but, as you add more water, it gradually becomes smoother and the lumps are fewer and larger. At the end, the mixture (or dough, as we now call it) forms into a single lump which you can take out of the bowl and hold in one hand. Its texture is smooth and its surface is dry and springy to the touch. It should not be sticky or wet. If it is, you have added too much water, so try adding more flour and mix well.

Sprinkle a little flour on the table or board and dust your hands with flour as well. This stops the dough sticking to your fingers. Put the dough on the table and knead it by pressing it flat with your hands, then folding it over to form it into a lump again. Do this for at least 10 minutes, so that plenty of air becomes trapped in the dough. Work really hard at this stage if you want a good loaf!

Kneading the dough

Put the dough back into the bowl and cover it with the cloth. Leave it in a warm place for about an hour. In this time the yeast will be producing carbon dioxide and the volume of the dough will roughly double. Meanwhile, rub a thin film of margarine all over the inside of the bread tin.

The next stage is 'knocking down'. Dust your hands with flour, then punch the top of the dough to make it smaller. Take it out of the bowl, and knead it for 2 or 3 minutes. Then work it into a shape suitable for the bread tin. It should be as long and as wide as the tin, but about half the height. If it is too large, tear off some pieces and roll them into balls (about 6 cm diameter) to make bread rolls. Put the dough in the bread tin, and put the tin on the baking tray. If you are making rolls too, grease an area of the baking tray and place the balls on this. Then cover the whole tray with the cloth and put it in the warm place again. It should stay there until the dough has risen to fill the tin. It may even bulge slightly over the top. This may take up to an hour.

About 15 minutes before the hour is up, turn on the oven and set it to 240°C (475°F, Gas mark 9), placing a shelf in the middle of the oven. When the oven has reached the set temperature and when the dough has risen, put the tray in the oven. After 5 minutes reduce the temperature setting to 220°C (425°F, Gas mark 7). Do not open the oven for 30 minutes at least. The loaf will probably be ready in 40 minutes, though may take up to 50 minutes.

When it looks fully baked, take it from the oven and turn it out of the tin, preferably on to a wire cooling rack. Knock on the bottom of the loaf with your knuckle. A 'hollow' sound confirms that it is properly baked. Wait for it to cool (if you can wait that long!) and it is then ready to eat.

MAKING A BREAD 'TIN'

The diagrams below and opposite show how to fold a piece of aluminium kitchen foil to make a baking tin which can be used once. Put the sheet on a table and mark the lines using a blunt pencil. Take care not to tear the foil. Each corner of the tin is made by folding as shown. Once you have got used to it, folding is easy. It is a good idea to try it first, using a piece of stiff paper of the same size. Fold so that points B and D meet each other, the foil being folded outwards along the diagonal line AE. Point A is carried around to meet with point C, but on the under surface of the foil. The foil may become rather crumpled while you fold it, but this does not matter. When the tin is formed, place each side in turn on a flat, firm surface and rub it smooth with a clean finger.

Making a bread 'tin'

Stage 1. Marking out the sheet of foil

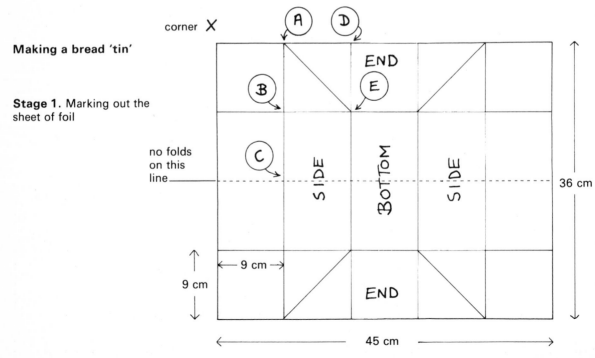

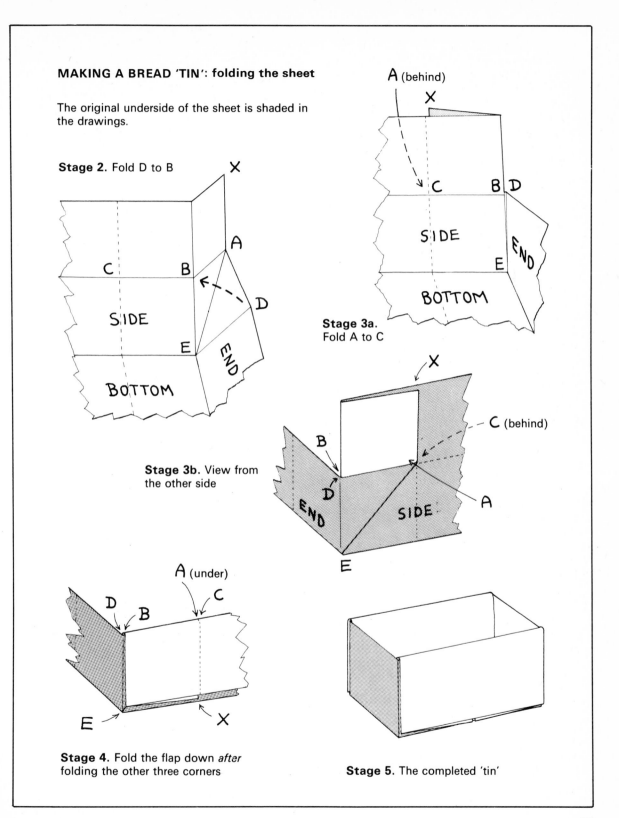

MAKING A BREAD 'TIN': folding the sheet

The original underside of the sheet is shaded in the drawings.

Stage 2. Fold D to B

A (behind)

Stage 3a. Fold A to C

Stage 3b. View from the other side

C (behind)

Stage 4. Fold the flap down *after* folding the other three corners

Stage 5. The completed 'tin'

8   Making wine

When we make bread (project 7) we knead the dough to mix air thoroughly into it and provide the yeast with plenty of oxygen. It respires and produces an equal volume of carbon dioxide, which leavens the dough. Yeast can also respire when no oxygen is present. Then it produces a little carbon dioxide and makes ethanol as well. Ethanol is one of the group of compounds known as alcohols. When we say 'alcohol' without saying which one we mean, we generally mean ethanol. The production of ethanol by yeast is called *fermentation*.

Using yeast, it is possible to ferment many different materials which contain a large amount of sugar, and which therefore provide the yeast with food. Fruits generally contain plenty of sugar. When fermented, each type of fruit gives its distinctive flavour to the product, which we call wine. Grapes are the fruit most often used for making wine, in Europe and other areas where the grape vine grows well. In other parts of the world, wine is made from bananas, the sugary sap from palm trees, rice, and many other sugary crops. A wine called mead can be made from honey which has a very high proportion of sugar.

Grapes are well suited to fermentation both because they are rich in sugars which the yeast can ferment, and also because wild yeasts grow naturally on the skin of the grape. Therefore, all that has to be done is to crush the grapes and strain off the sugary juice. This contains the yeasts from the skins that begin to ferment the sugars immediately.

The juice is held in air-free containers, so that ethanol is produced. Fermentation proceeds until the ethanol reaches a concentration that halts the yeast's activity in the juice. At that stage there may still be some unfermented sugar left, giving what is called a sweet wine. If there is little or no sugar left when fermentation stops, we call it a dry wine.

When fermentation is over, the yeast and fine particles of grape pulp settle to the bottom of the container. This material is called the lees. The wine is poured off from the lees and is usually filtered to make it clear. Then it is bottled. Often the wine is left for months or years before it is drunk. During that time, chemical changes take place slowly, which may improve its flavour.

Home wine-makers often use concentrated grape juice, which they buy in cans. In this chapter we see how to make wine from other kinds of fruit. These other fruits usually have less sugar than grapes, so we add ordinary sugar as well. Also important in wine-making are tannins. These help to improve the flavour. Without them, wines tend to have a 'flat' taste. The skin of grapes contains plenty of tannin, but many other fruits have little tannin. An easy way of providing a tannin is to add some tea. The quantities listed opposite are enough to make one bottle (750 cm^3) of wine.

GETTING STARTED

Wash all the equipment thoroughly in hot water. Then rinse it in cold water and let it drain. Take special care to clean the bottle: use a bottle-brush if you have one.

Put 600 cm^3 of water in the saucepan and heat it on the cooker. While it is heating, prepare the fruit.

If you use canned fruit, open the can, drain off the syrup and throw it away. Chop the fruit into small pieces (about 1 cm across) if it is not chopped already. Put the chopped fruit into the beaker.

If you are using dried fruit, chop every piece, that is, each raisin, sultana, currant, etc., into two or more pieces, and put them into the beaker.

Equipment

- Saucepan, to hold about 2 litres.
- Can-opener (not for the dried-fruit wine).
- Chopping board and sharp kitchen knife.
- Plastic beaker with a loosely fitting lid, to hold 1 litre. The beaker must be of white plastic, not of coloured plastic, and its inside surface must not be scratched or pitted. If your beaker does not have a lid, you need a sheet of polythene to cover the top and a rubber band to hold it in place.
- Lemon squeezer.
- Glass tumbler.
- Spoon for stirring.
- Straining bag or kitchen strainer. The straining bag is made of nylon or terylene. You can use a piece of nylon or terylene fabric if it has open weave of the kind used for plain net curtains.
- A wine bottle (750 cm³, sometimes labelled 75 cl; a centilitre is 10 cm³).
- Trap and stopper. The stopper must have a hole bored in it to fit the stem of the trap. Many forms of trap are available. The plastic type is cheapest and the least likely to break.
- Syphon tube. Plastic tubing about 8 mm in diameter and 1.5 to 2 m long. This is an optional item.
- Large funnel.
- A cork or plastic stopper for the bottle, if it does not already have a screw cap.

Ingredients

- A can (200 g size) of apricots (or peaches, plums, rhubarb, or almost any other fruit that you fancy). Apricots are recommended to begin with, as they ferment quickly. As an alternative which makes equally good wine, use 100 g of dried fruits, such as raisins or sultanas. The mixed dried fruit and candied peel sold as 'cake fruit' makes a really delicious wine.
- A banana (optional).
- A small orange and a lemon.
- 200 g granulated sugar.
- 50 cm (approximately) of cold tea; (you can use tea saved from the teapot).
- ¼ teaspoonful of dried yeast, or ½ teaspoonful of fresh yeast. Although special yeasts are sold for wine-making, ordinary baker's yeast is suitable.

Chop the banana into slices and add these to the beaker.

Cut the orange and lemon in halves. Squeeze one half of each and keep the juices in a tumbler until later. The unsqueezed halves are not needed for making wine. Take the squeezed halves and pare off the outer coloured skin. Put the pieces of skin into the beaker. Try not to cut off the white pith beneath the skins, for this gives a bitter taste to the wine.

Put the sugar into the beaker.

By this time the water should have boiled. Taking care not to splash it on yourself, pour the boiling water into the beaker. The heat of the boiling water sterilizes the beaker, the fruit and the other materials.

Stir the mixture until all the sugar is dissolved. Then add the cold tea, and the lemon and orange juices.

Put the lid on the beaker, or fix the polythene sheet across the top. Put the beaker in a warm place. It might stand in an out-of-the-way corner of the kitchen, or in an airing cupboard.

When the mixture has cooled to blood temperature or below, sprinkle the yeast into the mixture and cover the beaker again.

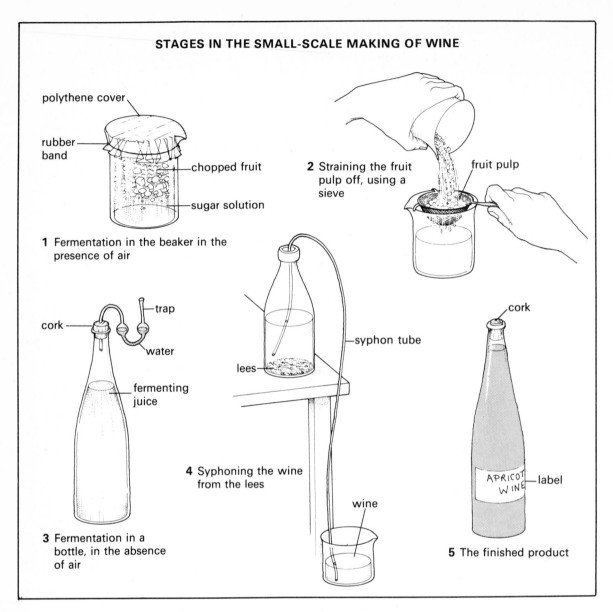

STAGES IN THE SMALL-SCALE MAKING OF WINE

polythene cover

rubber band

chopped fruit

sugar solution

1 Fermentation in the beaker in the presence of air

2 Straining the fruit pulp off, using a sieve

fruit pulp

cork

trap

water

fermenting juice

lees

syphon tube

4 Syphoning the wine from the lees

wine

cork

APRICOT WINE —label

5 The finished product

3 Fermentation in a bottle, in the absence of air

WHAT TO DO NEXT

At this stage, oxygen is available to the yeast, so little ethanol is being produced. The yeast is softening the fruit, allowing the sugars and flavours to pass into the liquid. The mixture may froth quite a lot. Uncover the beaker each day and stir the mixture for a minute or two.

On the fifth day, you will need another clean beaker, similar to the one you already have, or you can use the saucepan. Hold the straining bag or sieve in the second beaker and pour the contents of the fermenting beaker into the bag. The liquid runs through the bag, which retains the pulp. Hold up the bag so that all the liquid runs through. When most of the liquid has been strained off, squeeze the pulp to extract a little more liquid.

Throw away the pulp. Pour the liquid into the wine bottle. If it does not fill the wine bottle to the level shown in the drawing, add a little tap-water, warmed to room temperature.

Wet the tube of the trap and the hole in the stopper. Carefully push the tube into the hole, using a twisting motion. If you are using a glass trap, take care, for it could break. It is best to wrap it in a thick cloth such as a duster and hold it by this. Half fill the trap with water, as in the drawing. Then push the stopper firmly into the neck of the wine bottle.

Put the wine bottle in the warm place. The trap allows carbon dioxide to bubble out of the bottle, but prevents air from getting in. Fermentation is taking place and ethanol is being made. This process may take up to 3 months to complete.

fully pour off the wine, leaving as much as possible of the lees in the bottle.

A few teaspoonfuls of the wine should be tasted at this stage. If it tastes too dry, dissolve a little granulated sugar in it. If it has a sharp taste, this will probably go after the wine has been stored for 2 or 3 months. If the taste is good, there is no reason why it should not be sampled straight away after bottling.

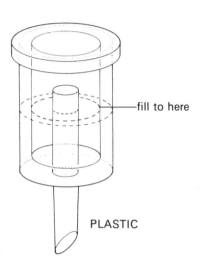

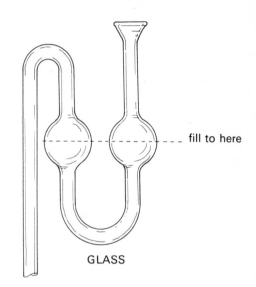

Types of trap. Traps similar to the glass trap are also available made of plastic.

RACKING AND BOTTLING

When fermentation is complete, you will see no bubbles in the wine or the trap. The yeast and other material settle to the bottom of the bottle, forming the lees.

The next stage is racking, in which the wine is syphoned off. Put the wine bottle on the table and the beaker on the floor beside the table. Fill the syphon tube with water and hold a finger over both ends. Put one end into the wine as you remove the finger from the other end. Do not let the end in the wine come close to the lees. Hold the other end in the beaker and remove your finger from that end. The wine now syphons into the beaker. As the level of wine inside the wine bottle falls, keep the end of the tube just below the surface. Towards the end, tilt the wine bottle slightly forward so as to make the wine deeper. Take care not to suck up any of the lees. If you find it difficult to syphon the wine, let it stand until the lees have settled, then slowly and care-

Wash out the wine bottle and pour the wine back into it, using the large funnel. If you are using a cork, soak it in water, then use a mallet to drive it into the neck of the bottle. It is far easier to use a bottle with screw stopper. The only danger with screw stoppers is that if the wine has not finished fermenting when it is bottled, the yeast may make more carbon dioxide and the bottle may explode under the increased pressure. Plastic caps are sold which snap into the neck of the bottle. These are cheap and will pop off if gas is produced.

Label the bottle with the name of the wine and the date on which it was bottled.

Store it in a cool place in which the temperature remains steady. A cellar is ideal, but a larder with north-facing window is almost as good. If you have used a cork, lay the bottle on its side to keep the cork moist. If not, stand the bottle upright.

If not ready for sampling immediately, the wine should be ready after a few months of storage.

9　Making beer

Once again we are making use of that small but extremely useful microorganism, yeast. As in the making of wine (project 8), we provide it with food in the form of sugar. A brewer uses the sugar from barley grain.

When it is harvested from the barley plant the grain contains mainly starch and very little sugar, so the sugar content is increased by *malting*. In the brewery the grain is spread out in flat heaps on the floor and water is sprayed over it. After a few days it begins to sprout. As this happens, the starch is being converted to sugar. Then the grain is dried to kill it. The dried sprouted grain is called *malt*.

Next the grain is ground in a mill and mashed in hot water to extract the sugar. The grain is then filtered off, leaving a solution known as *sweet-wort*, to which more sugar may be added. The sweet-wort is boiled to sterilize it and to make certain chemical changes occur. Now it is called *wort*. After cooling, yeast is added to ferment the sugars to produce ethanol.

An automated malting floor, where the barley is made to germinate. The machine to right of centre turns the grain over regularly. (Courtesy The Brewers' Society.)

WHAT YOU NEED

Equipment

- A saucepan, to hold about 2 litres.
- Plastic beaker and lid, as used for wine-making (see p. 31 for details).
- A spoon for stirring.
- A kitchen sieve.
- A wine bottle (750 cm³, sometimes labelled 75 cl), or glass bottle with a screw stopper which has a rubber or plastic sealer (fizzy drinks are sometimes sold in this kind of bottle), or beer bottle (1 pt, which will hold only 560 cm³ of the product). If the bottle has no really effective screw stopper, you will need a cork. If you know someone with a crown-corker, the best solution is to use a crown cork. (See the drawings below.)

Ingredients

- 750 cm³ water.
- 75 g soft brown sugar.
- 40 g dark dried malt extract.
- 10 g flaked barley.
- 2.5 g Fuggles hops.
- ¼ teaspoonful dried yeast, or ½ teaspoonful fresh yeast.

rubber washer
composition stopper

(a) Screw stopper   **(b)** Crown cork   **(c)** Ordinary cork   **(d)** Metal screw cap

Stoppers for beer bottling. (a) and (b) are best; (c) is satisfactory, (d) usually leaks.

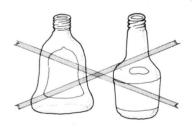

(a) Beer, wine and fizzy drink bottles   **(b)** Plastic bottles   **(c)** Fancy bottles, as used for spirits

Bottles for beer. (a) Strong, rounded, glass bottles are satisfactory.
(b) Plastic bottles may burst—DO NOT USE THESE.
(c) Fancy bottles may burst—DO NOT USE THESE.

35

At home we need not go through the complicated processes of malting. Dried malt extract, made by drying the wort and powdering the solid material which remains, can be bought for use in home brewing. It consists almost entirely of malt sugar, but also contains substances which give the malty flavour to the beer.

It is the custom to add hops to beer to give it even more flavour. Hops are the flowers of the hop plant. These are dried to retain their flavour, then added to the sweet-wort while it is being boiled.

Inflorescence of the hop plant

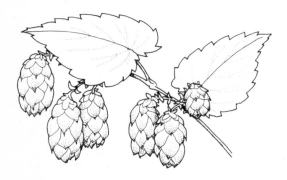

The recipe given here uses brown sugar as well as malt extract. This gives additional flavour and colour to the beer. The flaked barley adds a little 'body' to the product, which is best described as a Light Ale. The quantities given below are sufficient to make 750 cm³ of beer.

GETTING STARTED

Put the water in the saucepan and put it on the cooker to boil. While it is heating add: brown sugar, malt extract and barley.

The malt extract is a fine powder and, unless you take care, it rapidly spreads over a wide area. It then becomes very sticky and makes a horrible mess. Open the packet very gently and try not to spill any of it.

Stir the water to dissolve the sugar and malt extract. The malt extract may bob about on the surface in large sticky lumps, but these gradually disappear as the water becomes warmer.

When the water is boiling, add the hops. Stir for a moment to make sure they are wetted. Then put the lid on the saucepan, and turn down the heat so that it is just simmering.

Stir the mixture a few times every five minutes for half an hour. Make sure that it does not boil over. You may lose some water if it is simmering too fast, in which case add a little cold water to make up the loss. Next pour it through the sieve into the beaker. You may need help at this stage to hold everything steady. The sieve should catch all the hops and the flaked barley, which can then be thrown away.

Cool the mixture (or wort, as we may now call it) to room temperature. Do this quickly, by standing the saucepan in a sink full of cold water. But do not let it become too cool for this will slow down the beginning of fermentation. Put the beaker in a warm room, or in an airing cupboard, where it will not be disturbed.

Sprinkle the yeast into the wort. Put the lid on the beaker, or fix polythene sheet across the top with a rubber band.

WHAT TO DO NEXT

By the next day the yeast will have begun to ferment the sugars and a brownish foam will appear on the surface of the wort. Use the spoon to scrape away as much as possible of this. Look at the wort daily from then on.

READY FOR BOTTLING

When the yeast has fermented all the sugar, it becomes inactive and sinks to the bottom of the beaker. Before this stage is reached you will see a bubbly froth on the surface, telling you that carbon dioxide is still being made. When the froth clears and the solution itself begins to look less cloudy, you will know that it is ready for bottling.

Wash out another beaker or similar plastic container (or the saucepan). Without disturbing the yeasty sediment at the bottom of the beaker, tip the beer into the new container. (There will be a small amount of live yeast suspended in it.) You may have to leave a little of the beer behind in order not to carry over a lot of yeasty sediment.

Next, wash the bottle; use a bottle-brush if necessary, for it must be absolutely clean. Rinse it in cold water. It is usual for beer to be slightly fizzy, to improve its flavour. Since the yeast has already fermented all the sugar in the beer, it

Wort going into a copper tank, ready for fermentation. This is an old-style tank; modern ones are completely enclosed. (Courtesy Courage (Western) Ltd.)

needs some more sugar to ferment to make the fizz. Add a *level* teaspoonful of granulated sugar to the bottle. Do not add more than this, or too much carbon dioxide will be produced and the bottle may burst. Now fill the bottle with beer, leaving about 2–3 cm of air space above the beer. If you are going to use an ordinary cork, allow extra space so that there is a 2–3 cm gap between the bottom of the cork and the top of the beer.

If the bottle has a screw stopper, put this on now, making sure that it is completely air-tight. If you are using an ordinary cork, hammer it in with a mallet. Make sure that it is firmly in, or the pressure may blow it out again. A crown cork

is better, if you have access to a crown corker.

Put the bottle back in the warm room or cupboard and leave it for a week. In this time the yeast ferments the added sugar, making carbon dioxide to give the beer its fizz. Transfer the bottle to a cool place and leave it for 2 or 3 weeks. The remaining yeast settles to the bottom of the bottle and the beer becomes clear. It is then ready for sampling but improves slightly in flavour if kept a month longer. When the beer is being poured out, care should be taken to disturb the yeasty sediment as little as possible. If the bottle is tilted steadily, most of the beer can be poured off without carrying over much of the sediment.

10 Making yoghurt

Yoghurt is made by the action of certain bacteria on milk. They produce acidic substances in the milk, giving it a slight but pleasant sour taste. They also produce other substances which provide its distinctive flavour.

Yoghurt originated in the Middle East, where it is still widely eaten today. In warm countries, milk does not keep for long without going unpleasantly sour. The yoghurt organisms stop the ordinary souring bacteria from spoiling the milk.

By making milk into yoghurt it can be kept in a safe and edible condition for longer than raw milk.

Nowadays, lots of people in many countries throughout the world, including Britain, eat yoghurt regularly. Those who do not care for the flavour of natural yoghurt add chopped fruit, nuts or other flavourings to it. It can be used in savoury dishes too. It is easy to make yoghurt at home, as this project will show.

WHAT YOU NEED

Equipment

- *A saucepan to hold 2 litres, and lid.*
- *A thermometer (optional, see p. 42).*
- *Four containers to hold about 150 cm³ each: either use the plastic cartons in which yoghurt is sold, or use cups, mugs or tumblers. They need covers.*
  You can buy plastic drinking cups which have snap-on lids. If your containers have no proper lids, use small squares of food-wrapping film (Gladwrap, Clingfilm, etc.).
- *A warm box just big enough to hold the four containers when insulated. This is made by lining a wooden or cardboard box (or a biscuit tin) with sheets of expanded polystyrene (see p. 39). It is the extremely light solid substance (usually white) often used as a packing material around radios, TV sets and other fragile equipment to hold them safe inside their boxes. It can be cut with a sharp knife or sawn into sheets about 2 cm thick suitable for lining the box.*
- *A dessertspoon.*

Ingredients

- *600 cm³ (1 pt) pasteurized milk.*
- *1 carton of natural yoghurt.*

MAKING A WARM BOX

(See page 40 for an alternative design.) In choosing a box, make sure that when it is lined with polystyrene, the space inside will be big enough to hold your yoghurt cartons.

box or tin

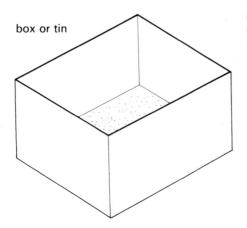

depth that allows
containers to
stand upright

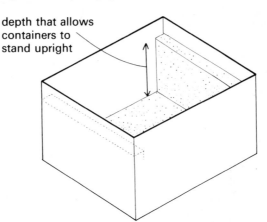

1 Cut a sheet of polystyrene to wedge firmly in the bottom.

2 Cut two pieces to wedge firmly in opposite sides. Leave a gap at the top.

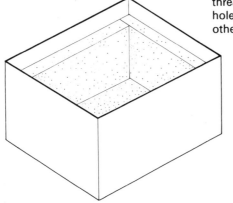

thread string through holes and knot on other side

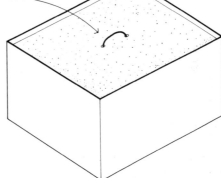

3 Cut two pieces to wedge firmly in the other two sides.

4 Cut a piece to drop loosely into the box. Put a string 'handle' on it.

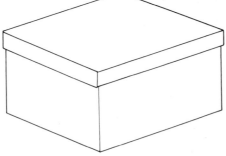

5 The box's own lid completes the warm box.

GETTING STARTED

It is best to begin in the morning.

Although the milk has been pasteurized, it still contains large numbers of the living bacteria which would make it go sour. You must kill these first. Tip the milk into a saucepan and put it on the cooker to heat. Watch it all the time while it is heating. Heat it slowly and, *just before it begins to boil*, take it off the heat. Put the lid on the saucepan to stop bacteria from getting in. Stand the saucepan in a sink filled with cold water.

An alternative warm box

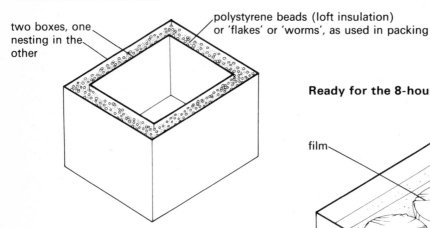

two boxes, one nesting in the other

polystyrene beads (loft insulation) or 'flakes' or 'worms', as used in packing

Swirl it around to cool the milk as quickly as possible. Feel it with your hands while it cools and stop the cooling when it is down to blood temperature. If you have the use of a thermometer, cool the milk until the thermometer reads 35°C.

Wash out the cartons, cups or mugs very thoroughly with hot water. Rinse them in hot water and stand them upside down to drain. While they are draining, open the carton of yoghurt and put one dessertspoonful of it into the warm milk. Stir well.

The yoghurt contains the living bacteria which act on milk to make yoghurt. There are two different kinds of bacteria and both kinds are required. The spoonful of bought yoghurt contains enough of both kinds to turn the warm milk into fresh yoghurt. You can eat the rest of the bought yoghurt.

Pour one quarter (150 cm³) into each of the containers and close them with their caps or film. Work fairly quickly so as not to let other bacteria into the milk and to avoid further cooling.

Now put the mugs into the warm box and put the lid on it. Of course, if you have a proper 'yoghurt maker', you can use that instead. The box is best stood in a warm room, preferably near or over a convector heater (a 'radiator'). The aim is to keep the temperature in the box as near to 35°C as possible for about 8 hours. It must not be allowed to get hotter than this for the bacteria will be killed. It does not matter as much if it becomes cooler, but the bacteria will take longer to turn the milk into yoghurt.

Ready for the 8-hour fermentation

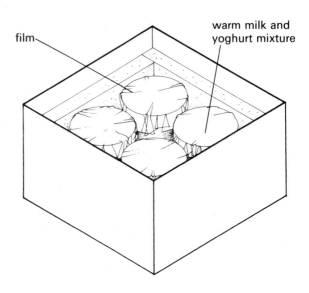

film

warm milk and yoghurt mixture

WHAT TO DO NEXT

Look at the yoghurt after about 8 hours. Do not take the caps or foil off the containers. Simply tip the containers slightly sideways to find out if the yoghurt has set. If not, put it back into the warm box and leave it for a few more hours. If it is ready, put the containers in a cool place, such as a larder or refrigerator. The yoghurt is ready to eat when it has been chilled. It should keep for 4 or 5 days in a refrigerator.

You can make more yoghurt, using your home-made yoghurt as a starter. This must be done while the home-made yoghurt is still fresh, within 4 or 5 days of making it. This applies only if you pay full attention to hygiene. Use fresh pasteurized milk. Wash all implements and utensils thoroughly before using them. Wash your hands too. Work carefully and quickly, keeping containers closed as much as possible. After a while, other organisms may find their way into the yoghurt; it is then necessary to buy another yoghurt from the shop. If you are in any doubt about the taste or texture of your home-made product, throw it away and start again.

YOGHURT SWEETS

Many people prefer to eat their yoghurt without adding anything to it. Natural yoghurt has a clean refreshing taste. The home-made sort lacks the sharpness that most shop-bought sorts have, and is generally pleasanter to eat. Many people like to add tasty things to the yoghurt after it is made.

Here are some suggestions:

Bananas	Dates	Jam
Strawberries	Raisins	Chocolate or
Hazel nuts	Walnuts	caramel sauce

You can stir in jams or sauces just before eating. To bring out the flavour of fruit or nuts, chop them finely, stir them into the yoghurt, and leave in a cool place for a few hours before eating.

YOGHURT SAVOURIES

Here are two suggestions:

Yoghurt potatoes. Boil small new potatoes, then chill them. Put them in a small dish and pour yoghurt over them. Stir to coat the potatoes with the yoghurt. This makes an appetizing side-dish to eat with cold meats and salad.

Curry. Yoghurt is used in traditional Asian cookery to marinate the meat or vegetables, and, added to the spices when cooking, it greatly enhances the flavour.

11 Making butter

It is not essential to use microorganisms for making butter. The cream of milk may just be churned until the tiny drops of fat come together in solid lumps. The fat is the butter; the watery liquid which is left is called *buttermilk*. To give butter a really good flavour, the cream is ripened *before* it is churned. This is done by adding a culture of special microorganisms to fresh cream and letting them live there for a while. They produce substances which give the butter a pleasant taste.

Home-made butter can be delicious—far nicer than most of the butters which you buy at the grocer's shop. It requires quite a lot of work, but you will also have learnt a lot by making your own butter.

WHAT YOU NEED

Equipment

- *Use of a refrigerator.*
- *A bottle of Milton.*
- *Two jugs, 1.2 litre size. If plastic, one should be boilproof.*
- *A tablespoon.*
- *A saucepan big enough to stand one of the jugs in.*
- *A thermometer, preferably a dairy thermometer. This is useful but not essential. The instructions advise you on how to judge the temperatures closely enough without a thermometer; the figures in brackets are for use if you have a thermometer.*
- *A kitchen mixer–beater with mixing bowl (unless you have a small churn, see drawing p. 44, or are willing to spend a long time stirring with a spoon).*
- *Cook's plastic spatula.*
- *Large plastic kitchen sieve.*
- *A plastic tea-tray.*

Ingredients

- *A culture of the butter-flavouring microorganism: the way to obtain and prepare the culture is described on p. 57. Prepare this a day or two before you intend to make butter.*
- *7 litres (12 pints) of Channel Island milk: this seems a lot of milk as it gives only about half a pound (225 g) of butter, but you cannot really use less. Since you need only the cream for making butter you will be left with about 5.8 litres of skimmed milk. This milk can be used for making curd cheese (about 1.8 kg), as described in project 12, or used in the ordinary way for drinking and cooking.*
- *Salt, a half teaspoonful.*

GETTING STARTED (FIRST DAY)

It is best to begin operations in the afternoon. *Read all the instructions first* to make sure that you will be able to do what is needed at the right times.

Check that there are at least four large ice cubes in the refrigerator and, if not, make some ice ready for the next day. The milk should have been delivered in the morning, so that by the afternoon it will have had time to stand and allow the cream to rise. Take the culture from the refrigerator and put it on the table to warm to room temperature.

for making curd cheese (keep it cool and use it the following day).

The next step is to pasteurize the cream by heating it to kill most of the microorganisms in it. Stand the jug of cream in a saucepan of water. Heat the saucepan, stirring the cream every few minutes. Every time you use the spoon for stirring, take it from the Milton solution, rinse it under the tap, stir, rinse it again, and return it to the Milton. Heat until the cream is *not quite* boiling (90 to 95°C) and keep it at that temperature for 30 minutes. Now cool it to room temperature (15 to 16°C) as quickly as you can. Stand the jug in a sink filled with cold water; stir the cream

Equipment for pasteurizing the cream

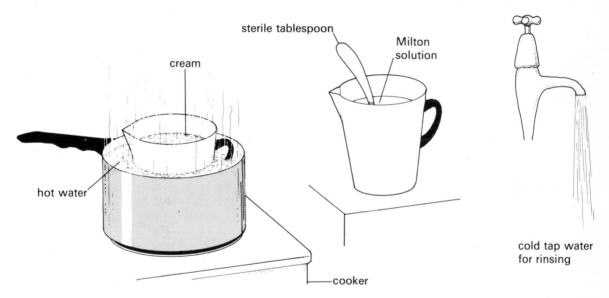

cream · sterile tablespoon · Milton solution · hot water · cooker · cold tap water for rinsing

Mix 1 litre of Milton solution in a large jug (see instructions on bottle). Let this stand for 10 minutes, swirling round occasionally to sterilize the jug. When you are ready to begin, pour the Milton into the other jug. Put the spoon in the Milton to sterilize it. Rinse out the empty sterilized jug with water from the tap.

Carefully open each bottle of milk and pour the cream into the sterilized jug—*do not shake the bottles*. Put each bottle gently down to stand. After you have finished, you may find that a little more cream has collected in some bottles. Add this cream to the rest. You should now have about 1.2 litres of cream and 5.8 litres of skimmed milk. Put the skimmed milk aside for kitchen use or

and swirl the jug around in the sink all the time. Stand the jug, covered by a lid or clean cloth, on the table and leave it for 30 minutes to come to room temperature.

Now the cream is ready to be ripened. Open the culture, scrape off the top 2 cm and throw this away. Stir the remainder, then put 6 tablespoonfuls of it into the cream. The rest of the culture can be used for making a new culture (p. 57). Cover the jug and leave it on the table until the next morning. If you are able to, stir the cream gently every hour or so. During this time the microorganisms are fermenting the sugars in the cream and making substances which will add flavour to the butter.

43

WHAT TO DO NEXT (SECOND DAY)

First thing in the morning, put the jug of matured cream in the refrigerator to chill it. It should have a cheesy smell by now. Do not worry if it seems to smell *too* cheesy. When made into butter it does not taste as cheesy as it smells now. It should have thickened during the night, but still be creamy, not set to a curd.

By the afternoon the cream should be cool enough for churning. This is best done in a cool room. The mixing bowl and beater should be cooled before use—put them in the refrigerator or rinse them in cold water. If you have a small churn like the one in the drawing, use it. If not, fit the beater attachment to the mixer. This is the attachment used in making bread and cakes, *not the whisk*. Pour the cream into the mixing bowl and set the mixer going at its slowest speed.

Nothing much happens at first, but be patient, for after a while you will begin to see tiny yellow specks of butter floating around in the cream. These specks are about 1 mm across and pale yellow. It may be 15 or 20 minutes before you see the first specks. Soon after that the number of specks increases more rapidly. As specks appear, use the spatula (sterilized in a jug of Milton solution, then rinsed) to scrape down any specks which get stuck at the edge of the bowl.

A domestic butter-churn

After about half an hour, stop the mixer. Now there should be masses of tiny specks of butter floating in a watery liquid. The watery liquid is much paler than cream, looking rather like milk which has had a lot of water added to it. This is the buttermilk.

Wash out the jug which held the cream. Put the sieve over that jug and pour the contents of the mixing bowl into the sieve. The specks of butter stay in the sieve and the buttermilk runs through into the jug. You can use the buttermilk for cooking. The butter should weigh about 450 g at this stage. If the liquid coming through the sieve is still very milky, and you get only a small amount of butter in the sieve, put the butter and buttermilk back in the mixer bowl and churn it a bit longer.

Separating the butter from the buttermilk

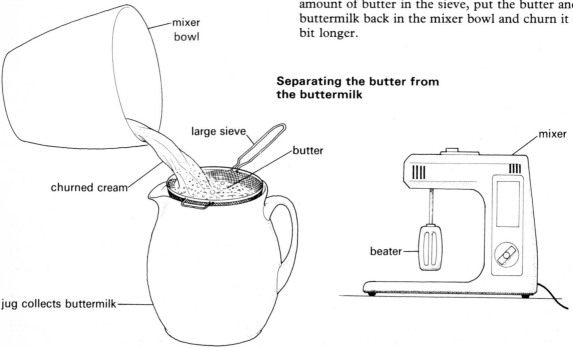

mixer bowl

large sieve

butter

churned cream

jug collects buttermilk

mixer

beater

When there is sufficient butter, put it back into the mixing bowl, add about 1 litre of cold water (2°C cooler than the butter) to it, and stir. This is to wash the buttermilk from the butter. Pour the mixture through the sieve again. Throw away the water which comes through. Repeat this operation using even colder water, 2°C cooler than the cold water and previously cooled by stirring two large ice-cubes into it until they have melted.

Tip out the butter on to a plastic tray, tilted as in the drawing. Sprinkle a half teaspoonful of salt on to the butter. *Wash your hands thoroughly*. Mix the butter and salt by hand, squeezing the butter to get rid of the last traces of water. The water runs down the tray and can be poured away. Gradually squeeze all the water out of the butter, which by now should be firm and a golden-yellow colour.

Shape the butter into a neat square block, using a knife or spatula, and put it into a butter-dish. It is ready for eating.

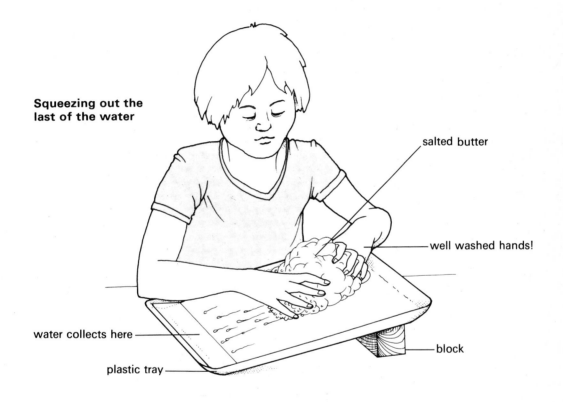

Squeezing out the last of the water

salted butter

well washed hands!

water collects here

block

plastic tray

Rules for success in making butter and cheese

1. Work in a clean room, preferably the kitchen. Wipe the working surface with a cloth soaked in Milton solution.
2. Use fresh pasteurized milk.
3. Sterilize all containers and implements just before you use them. Wash each item in Milton solution, and then rinse in cold water straight from the tap.
4. Leave empty containers covered or upside down.
5. Keep all containers covered during pasteurizing, cooling and ripening.

12 Making cheeses

Milk contains about 3 per cent of protein, which is in solution. Cheese is made from milk by causing the proteins to come out of solution and form a solid (or fairly solid) *curd*. The remainder of the milk is then called *whey*. Milk protein goes solid naturally when sour milk curdles. The curdling is caused by the acid made by microorganisms living in the milk. Cheese *can* be made from sour milk, but the taste is rather sharp. To make *curd cheese* we kill the microorganisms in fresh milk and then add a culture of special microorganisms. These organisms, too, curdle the milk, but in doing so they produce a much pleasanter flavour than that produced by the natural microorganisms of milk.

Another way of making the protein solid is to add an enzyme to the milk. We use the enzyme called *rennin*, which is taken from the stomach of calves and is then highly purified. When cheese is made in this way we add microorganisms to it as well. These grow in the curd, giving it a pleasant cheesy flavour.

The curd contains protein, some of the milk fats, and water. In making soft cheese we remove *some* of the water from the curd by straining it through a cloth. The cheese still contains about 60–80 per cent water. To make hard cheeses the curd is put under great pressure, which squeezes even more water from it. When it is finished, a hard cheese contains less than 40 per cent water.

In the first section of this chapter we make a soft cheese, using the acid produced by the microorganisms to cause the curd to form. A hard cheese made by using rennet is the subject of the second section of this chapter.

Making curd cheese

GETTING STARTED (FIRST DAY)

It is best to begin operations in the afternoon. *Read all the instructions first* to make sure that you will be able to do what is needed at the right times. Also read the rules to Section 2 on p. v.

Take the culture from the refrigerator and stand it on the table to warm up. Make up 1 litre of Milton solution by following the directions on the bottle. Put this in the bucket. Let the bucket stand with the solution in it for 30 minutes. Swirl the solution around from time to time to make sure the whole of the inside of the bucket is well sterilized. Then fill the jug with some of the solution and pour the rest away. Put the spoon in the jug of Milton solution, to sterilize it. Rinse the bucket with cold water from the tap.

The first step in cheese making is to kill the natural microorganisms by pasteurizing the milk.

Pour the milk into the bucket; stand the bucket in the saucepan, surrounded by water. Heat the saucepan until the milk is too hot to touch (74°C), but is *not boiling*. Stir it with the spoon while it is being heated. Every time you use the spoon, rinse it in cold water from the tap, use it, rinse it again, then return it to the Milton. Keep the milk covered while you are not stirring.

After half an hour remove the milk from the heat. Cool it as quickly as possible until it is warm to the touch (32°C) but not hot. The simplest way to do this is to stand the bucket in a large sink and run cold water around it. Stir the milk at the same time.

WHAT YOU NEED

Note. The quantities given are based on using the skimmed milk left over from making butter (project 11), but you can use half, a quarter, or as little as a tenth of these quantities to make a smaller batch.

Equipment

- *Bottle of Milton.*
- *Plastic bucket to hold the milk: this should be made of white plastic; the type sold for home brewing is suitable; it needs a lid or you can cover it by tying a sheet of polythene over it. Use a plastic beaker or china jug, if you are making a small batch of cheese.*
- *Jug, 1.2 litres.*
- *Tablespoon.*
- *Large saucepan big enough to stand the bucket in.*
- *A piece of cloth about 60 cm square; this should be fairly loosely woven.*
- *A thermometer, preferably a dairy thermometer.*
- *A length of strong string; about 2 m.*
- *A cook's plastic spatula.*
- *A supply of plastic food bags for storing the finished cheese (about eight bags, with ties).*

Ingredients

- *Culture of cheese-making microorganisms (see p. 57). Make this a day or two before you intend to make cheese.*
- *6 litres (about 10 pints) of ordinary milk or skimmed milk; the skimmed milk can be the milk left over from making butter (project 11).*
- *Salt, about 100 g.*

The next step is to add the culture of cheese-making microorganisms. Sterilize the spoon again in the Milton, then rinse it under the running cold tap. Open the culture and scrape away the top 2 cm of culture. Throw this away. Stir the remainder of the culture. Then add 4 table-spoonfuls of culture to the milk and stir well. The remainder of the culture may be used for making a new culture (p. 57).

Cover the milk and stand it in a warm room or in an airing cupboard (20–25°C) until the next day.

Equipment for pasteurizing the milk

plastic bucket   milk   sterile tablespoon   hot water   cooker

Milton solution   cold tap water for mixing

Tipping the curd into the cloth

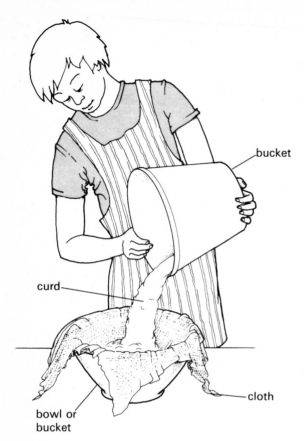

bucket

curd

bowl or
bucket

cloth

WHAT TO DO NEXT (SECOND DAY)

The culture needs to stand for about 20 hours in a really warm room or airing cupboard (25°C), but may need longer if it is a place which is not so warm (20°C). If you are in doubt about this, leave it until the third day before continuing.

The milk should by now have set to form a curd. This has about the same amount of stiffness as a rather sloppy jelly. If it appears to be ready, sterilize the cloth by boiling it in water for 10 minutes. Of course, the cloth must be washed first if it is at all dirty! Rinse the cloth in cold water and wring it out to remove as much water as possible. Spread it out in a large bowl, a large saucepan or in a plastic bucket similar to the one you have used for the milk. Carefully tip the curd into the cloth. Pick up the four corners of the cloth and tie them together firmly with the string.

Now hang up the cloth with the curd inside it and with the bucket beneath it to catch the dripping water. Leave it hanging until the next day. Every few hours take the spatula (sterilized in Milton) and scrape the curd away from the cloth. This mixes up the drier curd which is on the outside with the wetter curd which is nearer the centre, and helps the curd drain more quickly.

One way of supporting the curd while it is being drained

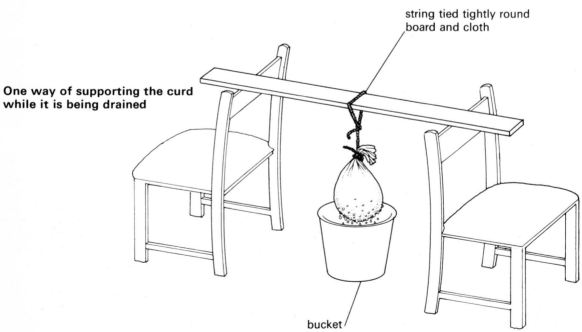

string tied tightly round board and cloth

bucket

48

FINISHING THE CURD CHEESE

The longer you hang the cheese the drier it will become. How long you leave it really depends on how dry you want it to be. After 2 full days at the most, it should be dry enough. Then take down the cloth, untie it and spread it out on the table.

The next stage is to salt it, but if you are going to use it for making cheesecake it should be left *un*salted. If you are not sure what you are going to use it for, it is best to leave it unsalted and salt it later if required. To salt the cheese, spread it out over the cloth and sprinkle salt on it. The amount needed is just under 50 g per kilogram of cheese. If you prefer it slightly salted, you need add only half or three-quarters of this amount. Sprinkle the salt over the layer of cheese, then mix it in well using the spatula.

This method gives about 1.8 kg of fairly moist curd cheese, or rather less if you let it drain for longer. Probably this will be more than you can eat or use immediately. The cheese can easily be preserved by deep-freezing it. Use a tablespoon (previously sterilized in Milton) to put the cheese into plastic food bags. You could pack it in quantities of, say, 250 g which is a convenient amount for most recipes. Seal the bags with the wire ties provided with bags, and place them in the deep-freeze compartment of the refrigerator. The cheese will keep for several months preserved in this way.

THINGS TO TRY

Curd cheese is delicious on its own, spread on cheese biscuits or on bread. To add variety you can mix other things in with the cheese. Try adding: chopped prawns, chopped onion or chives, chutney or pickles. Try anything else that you fancy, but first mix up a *small* quantity to make sure it tastes as good as you hope. If it does, you may have invented yet another type of curd cheese.

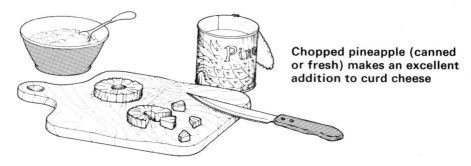

Chopped pineapple (canned or fresh) makes an excellent addition to curd cheese

Making hard cheese

There are many kinds of hard cheese. Cheddar, Double Gloucester, Cheshire and Wensleydale are just a few of many examples of hard English cheeses. These cheeses differ from each other according to the exact way in which they are made. Although the main stages are the same, there are differences in the quantities of ingredients used, the temperatures at which they are ripened, and many other differences of treatment which affect the final result. Even the size and shape of the cheese affect its flavour, for the ripening conditions in the centre of a small cheese will be quite different from the conditions to be found further away from the atmosphere inside a large cheese.

Most of the well-known hard cheeses *must* be made large and need to be put under very high pressure. It is not easy to make this kind of cheese at home with the equipment found in an ordinary kitchen. In this section we make a type of hard cheese known as Smallholder Cheese. It does not need a lot of milk or high pressures. It gives about 750 g of hard (or semi-hard cheese) very similar to the well-known hard cheeses.

WHAT YOU NEED

Equipment

- *Bottle of Milton.*
- *Plastic bucket with lid, as on p. 47.*
- *Large saucepan big enough to stand the bucket in.*
- *A jug, 1.2 litres.*
- *A tablespoon, a teaspoon and a cook's ladle.*
- *A thermometer (optional, see p. 42).*
- *A glass tumbler.*
- *A knife with a long wide blade: a proper curd knife or a ham carver.*
- *A piece of cloth, as on p. 47.*
- *Strong string, about 2 m.*
- *A cheese mould; if you are thinking of making lots of cheese it is worth while buying one but it is easy to make one which will last for a few cheeses (see drawings).*
- *A plastic tray.*
- *Pieces of muslin or cheesecloth; two pieces about 30 cm square and a strip about 0.5 cm wide and 60 cm long. The exact size depends on the size of the mould. You can use pieces torn from an old cheesecloth dress or shirt.*

Ingredients

- *Culture of cheese-making microorganisms (p. 57). Make this 1 or 2 days before you intend to make the cheese.*
- *6 litres (almost 10 pints) of pasteurized milk, freshly delivered.*
- *Rennet; the best is cheese rennet (supplier p. 58), but the smallest quantity you can buy is rather expensive for making just one batch of cheese. If you are thinking of making several batches or if you can share the rennet with others, the expense is more worth while. A much cheaper alternative is* Essence of Rennet. *You can buy this at a pharmacy or at a high-class grocery shop. A small bottle of essence is enough for at least one batch of cheese.*
- *Salt, 25 g.*
- *Cornflour, 2 teaspoonfuls.*

GETTING STARTED (FIRST DAY)

It is best to begin operations early in the afternoon. Read all the instructions first to make sure that you will be able to do what is needed at the right times. Also read the rules to Section 2 on p. v.

Take the culture from the refrigerator and stand it on the table to warm up. Make up 1 litre of Milton, following the directions on the bottle. Put this in the bucket. Let the bucket stand with the solution in it for 30 minutes. Swirl the solution around from time to time to make sure the inside of the bucket is well sterilized. Then fill the jug with solution and pour the rest away. Put the tablespoon in the jug of Milton solution, to sterilize it. Rinse the bucket with cold water from the tap.

For this cheese we can use milk which has been pasteurized at the dairy in the ordinary way. Simply open the bottles of milk and pour their contents into the bucket. Stand the bucket in the saucepan, surrounded by water (drawing p. 47). Heat the saucepan gently to warm the milk (32°C) but not make it hot. Stir the milk from time to time while it is warming. Keep it covered when you are not stirring it. When the milk is warm, take the saucepan containing the bucket off the cooker. Open the culture. Scrape away the top 2 cm of culture and throw it away. Stir the remainder of the culture and add 3 tablespoonfuls to the milk. Stir well.

Making a cheese mould from a white plastic bottle, such as a large cooking-oil or squash container.

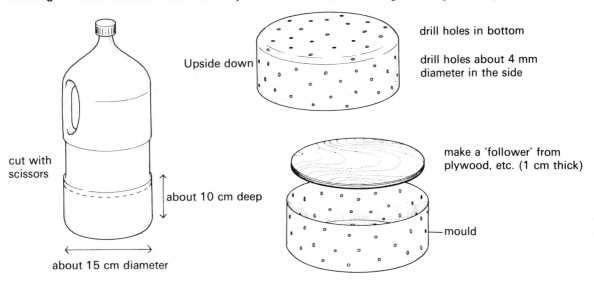

Upside down

drill holes in bottom

drill holes about 4 mm diameter in the side

make a 'follower' from plywood, etc. (1 cm thick)

cut with scissors

about 10 cm deep

mould

about 15 cm diameter

Cover the milk and let it stand in a warm room (20–25°C) for 30 minutes. This gives the micro-organisms a chance to begin growing in the milk. They will continue this growth all through the stages which follow, gradually adding to the flavour of the cheese. Towards the end of the half-hour prepare the rennet. If you are using cheese rennet, take 1 teaspoonful (5 cm³) of this and mix it in the tumbler with 4 teaspoonfuls (20 cm³) of water. The water should be *just* warm to the touch (about 35°C)—NOT HOT. When the half-hour wait is over, pour *half* the rennet mixture into the milk and stir well, using the table-spoon.

If you are using the Essence of Rennet, use 3 teaspoonfuls (15 cm³) of this, without mixing it

with water. The milk now has to stand for an-other 30 minutes to allow the rennet to form the curd. For the first few minutes stir the surface layer of the milk with a sterilized spoon to mix the cream with the milk below.

The length of time that the milk should stand depends on its temperature. It will not hurt to let it stand a little longer if you think that the rennet has not completed its work. When ready, the milk should have set to a smooth white curd. It has the texture of lightly boiled white of egg. Sterilize the long broad knife in Milton, then rinse it. Use it to make cuts through the curd about half an inch (1 cm) apart, slicing first one way, then the other (see drawings), and finally, turning the bucket, cut diagonally a few times. Then leave to

Cutting the curd

(a) Cut one way, knife vertical.   (b) Cut across, knife vertical.   (c) Cut with knife sloping at various angles.

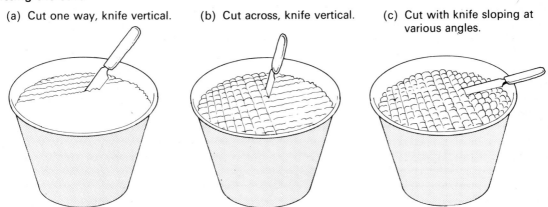

stand for 10 minutes. By this time you should see a little of the watery whey showing between the 'cubes' of curd.

Now put the saucepan containing the bucket back on the heat. Heat *very gently*, *stirring all the time*, to bring the milk up to blood temperature (32°C). This heating should take at least 15 minutes and perhaps up to half an hour. You must take special care not to let any part of the milk get hotter than blood heat, for this could kill the microorganisms from the culture and the cheese would not mature. It is very important to keep stirring while heating. During the heating the curd will become harder and be broken into smaller pieces. After 20 minutes, if the right temperature has been reached, remove the bucket from the saucepan and stand it on the table. Leave it there (with its lid on) for 20 minutes to let the pieces of curd settle to the bottom. The curd will then occupy about the bottom third of the bucket, with the whey occupying the top two-thirds. While the curd is settling, boil the large square of cloth in a saucepan of water for 10 minutes and sterilize the ladle in Milton.

Ladle off most of the whey. Rinse the cloth in cold water, squeeze it out and lay it in a bowl, a saucepan or another bucket (see drawing, p. 48). Pour the curds into the cloth. Tie up the cloth and hang it just as for soft cheese (p. 48). After 15 minutes, take it down and open the cloth. Cut the curd into slices and turn the slices so that the parts which were on the outside come towards the middle. Tie up the cloth again and hang it for another 15 minutes. Repeat this twice more. By now the curd should have rather a rubbery feel. Break the curd into pieces 1 cm across and add 25 g of salt. Mix the salt and curds together.

Put the mould on a tray and line it with the muslin or cheesecloth. Pour the curds into the cloth, press them down and wrap the edges of the cloth over the top. Put the follower on top,

The mould ready to receive the curd

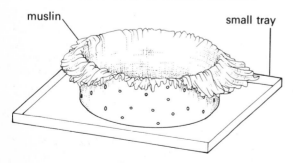

muslin

small tray

The first pressing

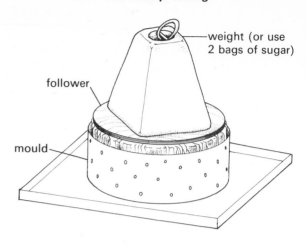

weight (or use 2 bags of sugar)

follower

mould

with a weight of about 2 kg. Leave this for an hour or two.

By now the pieces of curd will be sticking together to make a cheese, but handle it gently for it can still fall apart. Take the cheese out of the mould and unwrap it. Rinse the muslin; boil it for a few minutes; replace it in the mould. Put the cheese back in the mould *upside down* and wrap the muslin around it. Pull gently on the cloth to get rid of as many creases as possible. Put the follower on top and add a weight of 10 kg. Leave the cheese under this weight until the next morning.

If it happens that you are forced to finish for the day when the cheese is first put in the mould, you can leave it overnight like this. Then, first thing the next morning, change the cheese to the heavier weight as described in the last paragraph. It can be left like this until near the end of the second day, when it will be ready for the next step. The drawing on page 53 shows one way you can apply an increasingly heavy weight to the cheese.

WHAT TO DO NEXT (SECOND DAY)

Remove the cheese from the mould. Rinse the muslin and boil it for 5 minutes. While it is boiling, put the cheese into a bowl of very hot water (66°C). This is a little hotter than you can bear to keep your hand in. Leave it there for 20 seconds. Rinse the boiled cloth, put it in the mould and replace the cheese, upside down. This time put an even heavier weight on top. It should be about 20 kg. Leave the cheese for 24 hours.

large box

One way of getting a large weight for second and third pressings
Put water or stones or heavy metal objects in the bucket (1 gallon of water weighs 14 lb; 1 litre of water weighs 1 kg).

bucket leaning very slightly against the box

string to steady the bucket and stop it falling off

nail

follower

mould

Make cornflour paste by first mixing 2 teaspoonfuls of cornflour with *a little* water, to make a stiff paste. Then pour on a half a cupful of boiling water straight from the kettle, stirring well as you pour. Continue to stir for a minute. This makes a smooth stiff paste.

The cheese is now wrapped in the two squares of muslin. If necessary, cut them so they just overlap on the sides of the cheese. Put a square on each surface of the cheese. Turn the edges of the squares on to the edge of the cheese. Wrap the strip of muslin around the cheese to hold the squares in place. Fix the muslin in place by dabbing a little cornflour paste where needed.

FINAL PRESSING (THIRD AND FOURTH DAYS)

Take the cheese from the mould, rinse and boil the muslin. Replace the muslin and cheese in the mould (upside down). Put a weight of 40 g on top. If you cannot find such a large weight, put the biggest you can get. Leave the cheese for another 24 hours. By this time the cheese should be very firm, and it will begin to smell more cheesy, since the microorganisms have been at work for 4 days. If it is firm enough to handle (with care!), you can wrap it in muslin. If not, put it back in the press for another 24 hours.

MATURING

The microorganisms have still not had time to add the full flavour to the cheese, so it must be matured. Store it on a clean shelf in a room in which there are no flies or other pests. Every day, lift the cheese and turn it upside down. This stops the end resting on the shelf from becoming slimy. Continue this process for 2 weeks. Leave the cheese to mature for 1 or 2 weeks longer before you start to eat it. If you are maturing it in a cool room (10°C), such as a larder, it will need a few more weeks in which to develop its full flavour.

Wrapping the cheese in muslin ready for maturing. Trim the pieces of muslin to the right size and shape before wrapping.

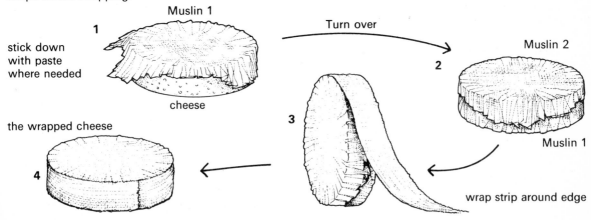

Muslin 1

1

stick down with paste where needed

cheese

Turn over

Muslin 2

2

Muslin 1

3

wrap strip around edge

the wrapped cheese

4

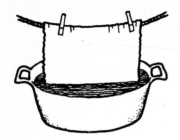

13 Colours from lichens

You can find lichens growing on stone walls, bridges and buildings, on rocks and cliffs, and on the bark of trees and shrubs. They are not common in towns because they are particularly sensitive to the pollution caused by smoke and the fumes from vehicles. In fact, the absence of lichens is sometimes used to indicate the level of atmospheric pollution. As might be expected, lichens grow best in country areas, particularly in regions most remote from towns, such as the Highlands of Scotland and the less inhabited parts of Wales, Devon and Cornwall.

A lichen consists of two kinds of very small organism growing together in partnership. The main body of the lichen consists of a fungus. Its hyphae are woven together to form a flat crusty growth, or a branching stem-like growth. The second partner is a single-celled alga, whose cells are held firmly among the woven hyphae. Like all green plants, the algae are able to take in carbon dioxide and water and to use the energy of sunlight to make these into sugars. Some of the sugars are passed on to the fungus partner as food. This is why the lichen can grow on bare

WHAT YOU NEED

Materials and equipment

- *A supply of lichens, preferably of several different kinds.*
- *Two or three small tubes or boxes (matchboxes) for collecting lichens in.*
- *A sharp knife or a pair of scissors.*
- *A pair of forceps (tweezers).*
- *Two or three test-tubes or boiling tubes and a test-tube holder.*
- *A small camping stove or other burner suitable for heating the test-tubes.*
- *Filter paper or fine sieve (optional).*
- *Some white unglazed fabric, such as cotton sheeting. A piece as big as the page of this book will be enough for many tests. Or you can use strands of white wool.*
- *A small saucepan.*
- *A few tablespoonfuls of vinegar.*
- *A packet of tartaric acid (Cream of Tartar), obtainable from a grocer.*
- *A packet of aluminium potassium sulphate (alum) obtainable from any pharmacist.*
- *Various other chemicals such as sodium carbonate (washing soda), potassium carbonate (you can use wood ash instead, as is used in traditional methods of dyeing), copper sulphate, and soluble salts of other metals such as iron, tin and chromium. It does not matter if you cannot obtain all of these. Even one or two will give you plenty of scope for experimenting.*

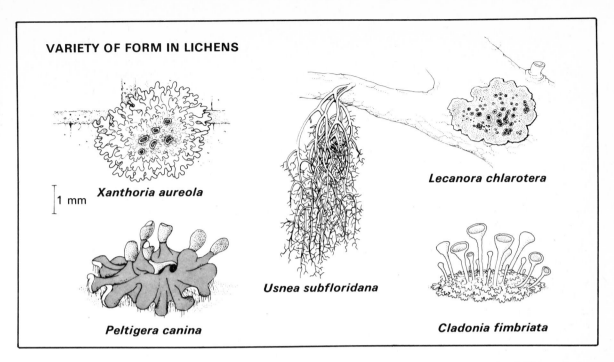

VARIETY OF FORM IN LICHENS

Xanthoria aureola

1 mm

Peltigera canina

Usnea subfloridana

Lecanora chlarotera

Cladonia fimbriata

rocks, where there is no other source of sugary food. In return for the supply of sugar, the fungus provides the alga with a support and a moist place in which to live. It may also absorb mineral salts from the surroundings and pass these to the alga. Different fungi are partnered with different kinds of alga.

For thousands of years people have obtained colour dyes from lichens. In Scotland and Ireland, lichens have been used to dye wool, giving the tartans and tweeds their characteristic range of colours. Unless you live in a remote area where lichens are really plentiful, you will not be able to obtain enough lichens to dye a garment, but you should easily be able to get enough to try out some interesting experiments.

GETTING STARTED

Lichens can be collected at any time of year, but the best time is autumn. It is best to collect in damp weather for the lichens are easier to gather when they are softened by moisture. You need about a matchboxful of each kind. Some lichens, such as the bright orangey-yellow *Xanthoria*, have bright colours in their natural state, but even those with dull greyish colours can give rise to quite different and interesting colours when suitably treated.

The lichens should be used within a day or two of collecting them. The general procedure for dyeing is as follows:

1. Chop up the lichen into small pieces with scissors or a knife.

2. Fill a test-tube about 2 cm deep with lichen, using forceps.

3. Add water (or other solutions, as will be described later) to a depth of about 4 cm.

4. Boil the water for 15–30 minutes. Take care that the lichen does not collect into a lump which spurts out on to the table and (possibly) your

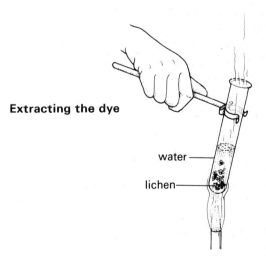

Extracting the dye

water

lichen

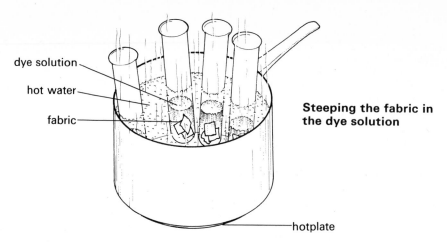

dye solution

hot water

fabric

Steeping the fabric in the dye solution

hotplate

fingers. The forceps can be used to break up any lump which tends to form.

5. Let the lichen settle to the bottom, then pour off the clear coloured dye solution into another tube. It does not matter if small pieces of lichen come over into the new tube. If you would prefer to have a really clear solution you can filter it through filter paper, or pour the cooled liquid through a fine plastic sieve. Throw away the lichen unless you think it possible to extract more dye from it, in which case repeat steps 3 and 4.

6. Cut small pieces of cotton fabric, about 1 cm square. You can use pieces of white wool about 5 cm long instead. If you like, you can use both cotton and wool, for the dye may work differently on each. Put the fabric or wool in the dye solution.

7. Stand the tubes containing the dye and fabric in a saucepan of hot water. Keep the water *just* simmering for 3 or 4 hours. Look at the saucepan at least once every half hour and add water to the tubes and to the saucepan if the levels have fallen. Sometimes it is a good thing if the dye solutions are not topped up at first. As the water evaporates from them they become more concentrated. This helps to dye the fabric more strongly.

8. Let the tubes stand overnight with the fabric in them to give the dye further time to work.

9. The next day, take the pieces of fabric out of the tubes, rinse them in cold water and place them on a piece of paper tissue to dry.

10. If you have kept notes of the lichen used, the solutions it was treated in (see below) and the times for which it was boiled and steeped, you could stick the dyed fabric or wool in your notebook beside the notes on how it was dyed.

DIFFERENT SOLUTIONS

The method described above can be altered in many ways. This is where dyeing becomes a real adventure, for there are so many things to try. One particular lichen found in Africa has become world famous as the source of litmus. Anyone who has ever done chemistry at school knows that litmus is used for telling whether a solution is acid or alkali. Litmus goes red in acid solutions and blue in alkaline ones. This is a clue to other ways of treating the dye solution. To make the solution acid, add a teaspoonful of vinegar to the water before you boil the lichen. In another tube boil the same lichen in water to which a pinch of sodium carbonate or potassium carbonate has been added. This gives a slightly alkaline solution. You may find that the lichen produces two entirely different colours. Do not expect bright strong colours from lichens. They usually give delicate shades.

Dyeing may be improved by adding chemical substances known as mordants. These help the dye to become attached to the fabric. This is something else to try. Alum is a mordant, so try adding a quarter teaspoonful of this to the tube before boiling the lichen. You can try adding alum alone or together with a small pinch of Cream of Tartar. If you keep notes and stick the dyed fabric in your notebook, you will soon discover the effects of these additional chemicals.

The salts of certain metals can also affect the colour given by the lichen. Try adding a small pinch of one of these to the water before you boil the lichen. You can try their effects with and without mordant and in acid or alkaline solutions. There is no end to the adventures with colours from lichens.

Cultures for butter and cheese

1. Buy a freeze-dried culture (supplier p. 58).
2. Sterilize a plastic container or wide-mouthed glass jar with Milton. Rinse it in cold tap water.
3. Put 250 cm³ of fresh milk into the container. Stand the container in a saucepan of water.
4. Heat to almost boiling (90–95°C) for 30 minutes. Then cool as rapidly as possible (25°C), as described on p. 43.
5. Add the freeze-dried culture and stir well with a sterilized spoon.
6. Put the lid on the container. Stand the container in a warm room or airing cupboard (25°C) until next day.
7. This culture can then be stored in the refrigerator for 1 or 2 days until it is needed.

The procedure above gives you the first active culture, which is then used for making cheese or butter or for starting other active cultures.

The way to use your active cultures is as follows:

1. Pasteurize 250 cm³ of milk, as in steps 2, 3 and 4 above.
2. Remove the active culture from the refrigerator. Use a sterilized spoon to scrape away the top 2 cm of culture. Throw away the scrapings. Stir the remainder of the culture.
3. Put 1 teaspoonful (sterilized spoon!) of culture into the pasteurized milk and stir well.
4. If the new culture will be wanted in a day or two, put it in a warm place as in steps 6 and 7 above. If the new culture will not be wanted for some time, put it in the deep-freezer. It can stay there for up to 2 months. The day before it is required, bring it out and treat it as in steps 6 and 7 above.
5. The remainder of the culture from step 3 may be used straight away for making cheese or butter.

Weights and measures

The quantities given in the various lists and instructions are in SI units. Since many readers will be working at home and may be using scales and measures calibrated in the British systems, a table of conversions is given below. For the purposes of the investigations and the recipes used in the book it is not necessary to use a precise conversion of SI to British units. The multiplying and dividing factors have been rounded off to make the arithmetic easier.

CONVERSION FACTORS

LENGTH		CAPACITY		WEIGHT	
Millimetres to inches	$\div 25$	Cubic centimetres (cm³)		Grams to ounces	$\div 28$
Centimetres to inches	$\div 2.5$	to fluid ounces	$\div 28$	Grams to pounds	$\div 450$
Centimetres to feet	$\div 30$	Cubic centimetres (cm³)		Kilograms to pounds	$\times 2.2$
Metres to feet	$\times 3$	to pints	$\div 560$		
		Litres to fluid ounces	$\times 35$		
		Litres to pints	$\times 1.75$		

SOME USEFUL BOOKS

These books will fill in the background details, to help you get more enjoyment from the projects.

Bonner, J. T., 'How slime molds communicate'. This is an article in *Scientific American*, August 1963; the Reference Department of your local Public Library may have a copy of this magazine.

Brightman, F. H. and Nicholson, B. E., *Oxford Book of Flowerless Plants* (Oxford University Press). The book is fully illustrated, so it will help you identify the lichens and the larger fungi.

Calder, R., *The Wonderful World of Medicine* (Macdonald).

Copland, A. (editor), *Mushrooms and Toadstools* (Blandford Press).

Finlay, W. P. K., *The Observer's Book of Mushrooms, Toadstools and Other Common Fungi* (Warne).

Finlay, W. P. K., *Wayside and Woodland Fungi* (Warne).

Hvass, E. and H., *Mushrooms and Toadstools* (Blandford Press).

Hastings, P., *Medicine—An International History* (Ernest Benn).

Moore, L., *Microscopes and Microscopic Life* (Hamlyn).

More, D., *Discovering Country Winemaking* (Shire Publications). A very inexpensive book with lots of tips and many recipes.

Parkinson, G., *Fungi* (A. and C. Black). An easy-to-use book with illustrated keys to help you find out the names of the fungi.

Rose, L., *Health and Hygiene* (B. T. Batsford).

Wells, A. L., *The Microscope Made Easy* (Warne).

ADDRESSES OF SUPPLIERS

Microorganism cultures for cheese and butter: Christian Hansen Laboratories Ltd., 476 Basingstoke Road, Reading, RG2 0QL (telephone 0734–861056). Ask for Dri-Vac Lactic Ferment. This firm also supplies cheese rennet.

Microscopes: A very inexpensive yet good quality ×40 fixed magnification pocket microscope is available from Starna Ltd., 33 Station Road, Chadwell Heath, Romford, Essex RM6 4BL (telephone 01–599 5116). It is sold under the name 'Micro Mike'.

A ×30 pocket microscope with built-in illuminator is available from Just Plastics Ltd., 5 Belgrave Gardens, London, NW8 0QY (telephone 01–624 3826).

Slightly more expensive, though having more refinements, are the microscopes from Bausch and Lomb U.K. Ltd., Highview House, Tattenham Crescent, Epsom Downs, Surrey, KT18 5BR (telephone 07373 60221). The Academic ESM 25/100 model is one of their cheapest and is very suitable for the projects described in this book.

The Griffin Minor Microscope (Griffin and George Ltd.—see below) has ×40, ×100 and ×200 magnifications and is of very high quality.

Microscopes, slides, hand lenses, biological instruments:

Griffin and George Ltd., 285 Ealing Road, Wembley, HA0 1HJ (telephone 01–997 3344).

Irwin Desman Ltd., 294 Purley Way, Croydon, CR9 4QL (telephone 01–686 6441).